The Good of This Place

The Good of This Place

VALUES AND CHALLENGES IN COLLEGE EDUCATION

Richard H. Brodhead

YALE UNIVERSITY PRESS
NEW HAVEN & LONDON

Marie Borroff's "In Range of Bells" is reprinted with permission of the poet.

C. P. Cavafy's "Ithaka" is reprinted from *Collected Poems*, rev. ed., ed.
George Savidis, trans. Edmund Keeley and Philip Sherrard, 1992.
Copyright © 1975 by Edmund Keeley and Philip Sherrard. Reprinted
by permission of Princeton University Press.

"On Administration" was originally published as "How I Spent My Summer"
in vol. 26, no.1 of *The New Journal*. Used with permission.

"An Anatomy of Multiculturalism" was originally published in the April 1994 issue
of the *Yale Alumni Magazine*. This piece was adapted from a talk delivered to the
October 1993 assembly of the Association of Yale Alumni. Used with permission.

The following essays were published previously and are used with permission:
"On Residential Education," "On Sexual Harassment," "At the Millennium,"
Yale Daily News; "Two Writers' Beginnings," *The Yale Review.*

Designed and set in Yale typeface by Gregg Chase.
Printed in the United States of America by Sheridan Books.

Library of Congress Cataloging-in-Publication Data
Brodhead, Richard H., 1947–
The good of this place: values and challenges in college education/
Richard H. Brodhead
p. cm.
ISBN 0-300-10600-9 (cloth : alk. paper)
1. Education, Higher—Aims and objectives. 2. Universities and colleges—
Administration. 3. Yale University. I. Title.
LB2324.B76 2004
378.73—dc22
2004002275

A catalogue record for this book is available from the British Library.

The paper in this book meets the guidelines for permanence and durability of
the Committee on Production Guidelines for Book Longevity of the Council on
Library Resources.

10 9 8 7 6 5 4 3

CONTENTS

PREFACE

BETWEEN 1993 and 2004, I held what I take to be one of the most interesting posts in American higher education: that of Dean of Yale College. The interest of the position is only partly a function of the school it serves. The intelligence, vitality, and generosity of the faculty and students I dealt with never ceased to amaze and delight me, and it was a continual privilege to work for a great university during a great period of rebirth. But beyond its location, a considerable part of the post's interest came from its peculiar structure.

At most other schools, one person would be responsible for faculty appointments, another for undergraduate curriculum, and a third — possibly minimally related to the rest — for questions of student life. At Yale, for historical reasons few can recall, these spheres are overseen in significant measure from a single position. The holder of this position has, in consequence, an almost unbelievably varied day, bouncing from conferences with architects on dorm renovations, to meetings with students — discontented or aspiring on any of a thousand fronts — to strategy sessions on building new faculty strengths, then on to considerations of athletics or admissions policy or international student aid, with the likelihood that at any moment, some unforeseen emergency will change the whole character of the day.

If one can tolerate the frequent and almost random changes of subject, the position has peculiar pleasures, and strong advantages as well. From the institutional point of view, this position has the advantage that it forces aspects of university life that belong together to be considered together. No danger, in this scenario, that the needs of students will be forgotten when faculty appointments are assessed. The two belong to a single portfolio. No danger that formal academic study and the further education derived from extracurricular life will be mistaken for separate processes. (They are continuous in the experience of students, though they are usually not administered that way.) Under this structure, the two are always coming up together, as separate phases of a single whole.

But if the unification of these fields has advantages for the school, the main advantage, I always felt, was to me. For although my work was heterogeneous and demanding, just for that reason the position afforded a magnificent education. To be Dean of Yale College was to have reason to meet all the different people who make undergraduate education happen. With their intricate internal divisions by department or support function, universities have something of the quality of a honeycomb, a whole built through the internal walling off of a thousand separate cells. But my role broke through every barrier, introducing me to the whole plenum of chemists, coaches, classicists, chaplains, computer scientists, career counselors, chamber musicians, and the rest (pick your letter and I could produce a comparable list) who, together, if often invisibly to each other, make the project of education work.

The acquaintance thus supplied was an endlessly rich reward; but a further benefit was more valuable yet. For the main result of the position's shape was to make you think: to force you to try to understand the separate goals of the university as well as the whole they formed. Through the division of labor all academics and university employees take for granted, the jobs of the university's parts are typically pursued in isolation, with little invitation to think of distant parts and little pressure to grasp the deep goal they all serve. It was the nature of my job to require me to think how each part of the college contributed to the central mission: furthering knowledge and training young minds.

This book is a collection of writings that I produced in my role as dean. They reflect their occasions, and therefore show the marks of their place of origin. But their bearing, I trust, is by no means confined to Yale. Beneath the tissue of local reference, these pieces grapple with central issues of undergraduate education: no one school's monopoly, but problems widely shared.

The works in the first section, talks composed for the Freshman Assembly where Yale College welcomes new students, try to say what college is good for and how students can get the good of it. In the frenzy that surrounds selective college admissions in our time, the pressure to get into a top school is so great that little time is spent asking what this all-desired thing is really about. These talks were my effort to provoke reflection at a strategic moment in students' lives, and, if not to dictate, then at least to inform and enrich the terms on which they would engage their new world.

The later sections range through familiar challenges of the contemporary university, from free speech and diversity issues to sexual harassment policy to the complex and competing goals of college admissions to the question how the modern curriculum, a multiverse of specialized offerings, can be made to yield a coherent education.

These statements were all issued from an official position. But to think of them as official pronouncements would be to miss their character and, to my mind at least, most of their interest. As I review these pieces, what strikes me is how much they embody my own education: the ongoing struggle for understanding that the deanship required and enabled. These are, unmistakably, teaching pieces. (I have never regarded work in university administration as anything but an extension of the work of teaching.) But they are also, almost every one of them, efforts at self-teaching: efforts to express, and thereby better understand, the deep values of undergraduate education.

People are always running up to college officials in highly fraught situations and asking what the institution's position is on some vexed issue. They do not always realize that, though universities of course have policies, they do not have playbooks that tell what's right to do in each complex and unforeseen circumstance; nor is there a dean's answer sheet to explain the philosophy that guides a hard decision. The answer has to be made up on the fly, and in the heat—and to arrive at an answer, the complexities of the question have to be worried at and worked through. These pieces embody the kind of act of thinking that my role forced on me.

To go back through these writings is to be vividly reminded of the hundreds of colleagues and students I dealt with as dean and how much I learned through our work together. I would rejoice to name them, but the list is just too long. They are not acknowledged on this page but they are acknowledged in my heart.

I must make an exception for a few people whose contribution to my work was fundamental. Joseph Gordon, wisest and most reliable of colleagues, lent hourly guidance from his role as Deputy Dean. Betty Trachtenberg, tough when toughness was needed but eager to help with every good student initiative, was my daily tutor in the support of student life. Penelope Laurans's irrepressible energy, enthusiasm, and dedication were essential to the success of my largest single undertaking, the 2001–3 review of Yale College education. My assistant Lorie Fontana kept calm through every crisis and helped me at every point.

In the larger university, two provosts, Alison Richard and Susan Hockfield, gave excellent support to the college and became extraordinary friends. Peter Salovey, a later addition to our administrative cadre, brought fairness, discernment, practical intelligence, and good humor to every challenge. As for Rick Levin, who assumed the presidency of Yale the same day I took on the role of dean, I could not have asked for a warmer supporter of every good thing I tried to accomplish — or a more generous colleague and friend. I have Howard Lamar to thank for appointing me to this position while he was Acting President and for supplying a noble model from his own days as Dean of Yale College. I thank Charles Ellis and Linda Lorimer for many things, not least their role in the creation of this book.

Yale has been the scene of my education for many years. But the point of college is to give such exercise to the powers — not just to academic intelligence but to human intelligence in the broadest sense — as fits people to live constructively in the world.

My own rather protracted time in Yale College, above all the education I received as dean, has equipped me too to graduate and move on — in my case, to the new challenges of another great role in American education, the presidency of Duke University.

I thank everyone who played a part in my Yale education. I leave to continue the work of education — my own not least — at Duke.

> Richard H. Brodhead
> New Haven, Connecticut
> January 2004

WORDS FOR
NEW STUDENTS

WELCOME HOME

Freshman Address, August 28, 1993

PARENTS, COLLEAGUES, and Men and Women of the Freshman Class: It is an enormous pleasure to welcome the Class of 1997 to Yale.

I look out at you and see a group of people literally in suspense, between settled states. You have recently been at home in one or several kinds of homes (a family, a school, a community), but you have moved away from them in coming here. Soon enough you will have made a new home at Yale, but you are not at home here yet. Such a state invites meditation on what a home is, and what it means to be at one. A home — to begin — is a constructed thing, something we have to build and hold in existence, not something furnished us by nature. It is a physical but also a social space, a world we compose together in which things feel familiar; congenial; knowing of our natures and responsive to our needs. But if a home is a built thing, it is also built over against. It is in essence a defensive structure, something contrived to shield us from things we would otherwise be all too obviously exposed to — vulnerability, loneliness, alienness, and the rest. So a home is in the deep sense of the word a security system: a world of belongingness thrown up against a larger world of exposure and strangeness.

Since a home is a protective structure, it is no wonder that we — poor, bare, forked animals that we are — crave one, and that we strive with strong instinctual force to build a new home when an old one has been damaged or destroyed. But it is just the fact that a home is a protective device that also makes our

3

experience of it fundamentally ambivalent, and makes the "homey" carry the opposite meanings at once of something secure and something much too secure—a place where things are familiar, and so of belongingness, but also a place where things are all too familiar, and so of blandness, tameness, or monotonous sameness; a place where we are sheltered from a menacing outside world, but also a place where we are "sheltered" in the sense of shut in, insulated from excitements and challenges we might well want to face. (No one I know has aspired to have this epitaph: "He Led A Sheltered Life.")

I do intend to draw a moral from these reflections, and here it is. If I can say one thing to you on the occasion of your entering Yale, it is to exhort you to remember the double meaning of "home" as you build a home at Yale. In the deepest sincerity I say to you, Please make yourself at home here; and with equal but countervailing earnestness, Please: as you do so, don't be too addicted to the self-limiting pleasures of security.

Let me try to focus this message into two more practical applications, the first one very practical indeed. You came here, I assume, in order to get an interesting education. We all know how easily that larger ambition can decline into the lesser exercise of picking courses and filling up a program, a means to education that always threatens to become treated as if it were the end. But we sometimes witness a further degeneration, in which the most capable young men and women in America, having arrived in a university offering truly multitudinous educational enticements, set about composing a program as a kind of exercise in self-protection. You may not believe it, but I have actually encountered arriving freshmen who act as if the greatest privilege Yale offered were that of letting them at last discontinue unpleasing forms of study, and who blandly offer, as adequate reasons for avoiding whole realms of knowledge for the rest of their lives, profundities like "I'm not a Math person," or "I'm just not good at languages," or "I read some poetry and didn't like it," or "I already studied science in high school." Let me invite you to the idea that such diagnoses are acts of self-limitation trying to pass themselves off as acts of self-knowl-

edge, and that they embody home-building in the destructive
sense: an effort to hole up inside the area of an already-certified
competence and so to minimize the dangers of exposure.

If no one has done so already, let me be the first to tell you
that this impulse toward self-protection is completely natural
and highly understandable, but also devastating to the project
of education; and that the way to get the good of this place is to
stretch yourself, to expose yourself to what you don't already
know and aren't already good at. Emily Dickinson, who entered
the freshman class at Mount Holyoke 145 years ahead of you, in
1848, wrote to a college friend in 1850: "The shore is safer,
Abiah, but I love to buffet the sea," and you too can think of
more valuable goals for your education than an unadventurous
safety. Yale's distributional requirements try to mandate a certain amount of exploration and curricular adventuring from
you, but institutionally Yale can only express its hopes for you
negatively: by saying You can't not have taken three courses in
each of the four divisions by the time you graduate, You can't
not take two courses from Groups One and Two and two from
Groups Three and Four by the end of the first year, and other
dicta sounding like the rules of an unpleasantly complicated
board game. We count on you to realize the spirit within the
letter of these laws and to convert their negative phrasings into
the positive they are meant to foster — the effort to keep opening
yourself to what you have not yet faced, to keep pressing out
beyond wherever you have become at home.

Let me now redirect my homily against homebodyism
toward another area of your coming education, your life
together. Anyone with any powers of empathy will be able to
remember the social condition you find yourselves in today (am
I wrong?): in the state, alternately very exhilarating and very
depressing, in which every person you meet is another stranger
and each possible relation has to be built up from scratch. Easy
to understand the acts of reconnaissance, in such a situation, by
which we scan the world of strangers for those "like us," in
hopes of recruiting them into a personal set and reassembling a
familiar home. But I wonder if I am the only one here who has

also felt the relief—available in your current situation—of *not* being known, the exhilaration of not having to be taken for (just) the person we have been known as in the last chapter of personal history, and so of being free to put forth a new self not yet fixed by received identifications? No one will block you in, and you will find much official encouragement for, the effort to reconstitute already-established communities, organized around any dimension of perceived likeness, on this new ground. You will find that one glory of this university lies in the variety and vitality of the communities that thrive within it. At the same time, let me implore you not to be too addicted to the comforts of homogeneity and social self-enclosure—not to miss those opportunities for enlarged knowledge and self-knowledge that can be derived only by lifting identifying labels off of yourself and others and going out into worlds (nominally) "other" to your own.

At stake here is the quite local question of how you arrange your daily life; but I give the point emphasis in the belief that such personal issues link up with larger problems of our world. We can't be sure how the history of this time might eventually be retold, but from the vantage of the present two historical developments are especially striking in the years of your early adulthood: first, the unanticipated and unforeseeably rapid collapse of the collective identities that held the international world in fixed, coherent shape from the late 1940s on through the late 1980s, the great Cold War oppositions of Free World vs. Communism (or alternatively of Socialism vs. Capitalism) that built a sense of national purpose within the United States and the Soviet Union and arrayed other nations in alliance around them; and second, the even more unforeseen fact that the easing of Cold War global oppositions should have resulted in the resurfacing of bitter, nasty local conflicts, conflicts based on the sort of passionate local loyalties and animosities the great global oppositions of midcentury made seem to have been superseded. The collapse of post–Cold War Yugoslavia into warring Serbs and Croats and Bosnian Serbs, Croats, and Muslims provides us with the most conspicuous example of this process, but almost any country will furnish parallel examples:

as Czechoslovakia, held together as a national entity by the Warsaw Pact alliance, has split with the waning of Russian power into separate nations of ethnic Czechs and Slovaks, with Slovakia now in turn agitated over the rights of its ethnic Hungarians; or as Germany, fixed in a state of separation by the Cold War map of Europe, has been rejoined politically only to suffer social antagonism between West and East and by both against various immigrant groups.

Our own recent history is not identical to these, but it is not without analogies. In the wake of what I take to be the great transformative event in the American life in the second half of this century, the Civil Rights movement and its still-vigorous offshoots, group after group — grouped by race, gender, physical disability, and sexual preference — has successfully dramatized the fact of its exclusion from full citizenly life, its members identifying themselves more tightly *with* the group the better to counter the fact of its exclusion. In consequence, at the same time that it has become more committed to the general idea of social inclusion, American society has become in practice more segmented in recent years, more organized around partitive social allegiances and correspondingly weaker in collective aims. (Might one not conclude on a bad day that the main "common" sentiment shared by Americans — not least by Americans with excellent educations — is the one the novelist Henry James formulated in 1905? "To make so much money that you don't 'mind,' don't mind anything — that is absolutely, I think, the main American formula.")

We do not live — though much of our world does — in the state of civil war. But in the hardening group identities in our time we perhaps already experience a taste of what the poet Yeats named as the emotional residue of civil war:

> We have fed the heart on fantasies,
> The heart's grown brutal from the fare;
> More substance in our enmities
> Than in our loves.

And this fact of partitive local division, I would propose – what the philosopher-critic Cornel West calls "this failure to connect [that] binds us even more tightly together" – sets the outer horizon your life here must be plotted against. A great task of your time, one great need of the world you will go forth to shape and to serve, is to figure out how to escape from the oppressions of oppressive collectivities without recoiling into the bad polarities of sectarian or partisan self-assertion; to figure out how, in full consciousness of the ways so-called common identities can exclude and subordinate, to forge that new shared, *common* sense within and only within which difference can be protected and made creative.

You come here to a place full of diversity. I ask each of you, in the way you organize your engagement with this multiform human world, to take seriously the notion that you could be helping create a model or exemplary community: helping to design habits of collective association badly needed in the world at large. Officially Yale can only define your conduct in terms of what you must not do. It is for you to work out the positive con-tent of a proper community. Obvious suggestions would be that you not coerce one another; that you not intimidate one another; that you practice tolerance and respect for one another (not just when it's easy) – but these are paltry, minimal requests. The more exciting hope would be that you would be not just respectful in the face of each other's difference but actively, mutually inquisitive: willing to open yourself to what seems foreign and so to overcome the insularity of each homebound life.

What has brought you here together? The fact that you are smart, I know; self-disciplined, for sure; ambitious, a fair bet; eager to serve others with your intelligence, I trust. But this is above all a place of inquiry; and what has most profoundly qualified you to come here is an ardent curiosity – a passionate will to know and understand. If that is so, I can sum up my exhortations by urging you to keep in touch with your curiosity during your time here, and to insist on your right to free exploration against every possible inhibition from without or from within. The peculiarity of this home you have come to is that it protects you best when it exposes you most fully, and that you most truly inhabit it not when you stay in the familiar but when you venture outside the already known. On that understanding, that what you have come here for is really to learn a little, from every intellectual and social source that will now surround you, I can say the short version of these longish remarks: Welcome home.

THE FREEDOM OF THIS PLACE

Freshman Address, August 27, 1994

MR. PRESIDENT, colleagues, parents, greetings. Excuse me if I address my remarks to the impressive group before me, the new recruits to Yale College.

You may think that this is a merely ceremonial occasion, a chance to overawe you with monumental architecture and academic finery. My own guess is that this assembly has a serious function: not just to let you see yourself as a class, but to remedy a slight defect in the Yale admissions process. While at this time last year you looked to colleges merely as anxious hopers, and whereas now you're not just "in" but so convincing-looking as to seem to deny that there was ever any doubt about it, it may have occurred to you that the moment never arrived that you could point to and say: "That's when I became a Yale student." Once upon a time you had applied here, but you weren't in yet. Then you were admitted, but you still weren't here yet, and still knew little enough what awaited you. Then you arrived, but in the bustle of unpacking you'll have been highly aware that Yale hasn't started yet. Soon it will have started, but then you'll be too busy for reflection until the day you realize that you're already quite at home here. So it is that the climactic moment, the instant when you entered Yale, will seem first to be still ahead of you, then already behind you, without having actually taken place.

To those of you for whom this has been a problem, good news: our convocation exists to remedy this deficiency. For the one serious business we can transact this afternoon is to appoint some exact minute as the time when you leave old identities behind and become full citizens of this place. Let's say that time is now.

Men and Women of the Class of 1998, welcome to Yale College.

This concludes the business portion of our program, but don't leave quite yet. I'd like to commemorate this moment by saying a word about this place and what you are in for.

When I ask myself what a school like Yale is for, many answers come to mind, but the profoundest one I can think to give is that this school exists to offer a highly unusual experience of freedom. The surly among you might be heard to mutter: "What do you mean, freedom? What has my life been since I got here but a continual exercise in obligation? What have I done so far but meet the rigorous schedule set forth in the "Calendar of Opening Days," and what done in my leisure but read the *Undergraduate Regulations* — all 111 pages of them? What do I have in prospect but four years of obeying these regulations (you'd better!) and trying to comply with the intricate legalisms of the *Yale College Program of Study:* taking no fewer than two courses from this group, no more than six from that group, and so on? You call that free?"

I do. Your life here will indeed not be one of unconditional or unqualified freedom (no life is), but it will be lived under conditions rarely encountered elsewhere. First, you are embarking on a life in which many kinds of familiar restraint will be mysteriously alleviated. You will be out from under the surveillance of those loving regulators who have watched over you heretofore: you'll have no one to ask whether you made your bed or finished your homework, no one to tell you when it's time to get up or to ask when you came in last night. You will have the profound freedom we lose when we enter the world of work, the freedom to be master of your day and to do what you have to do when you choose to do it. You'll be free here to say what you think, and indeed to think what you think. Since this is a luxury by no means universally enjoyed, we would do well to stop and remind ourselves of the good fortune that removes us from the physical coercion and intellectual and emotional intimidation that govern the life of so many fellow humans. You'll be free from those forces here, but free too from the limits that social homogeneity can create even in peaceable worlds — worlds where speech and thought are not forbidden, are even valued ideals, but where nothing stimulates the actual activity of free thought or speech, since people live in such a high state of mutual agreement.

With such constraints suspended, you are entering a world where you will be surrounded by an almost uncontrollable pro-liferation of activities soliciting your interest and involvement. You must take courses, it's true, but something like 1,800 courses offer themselves for your election each year. If this menu proves too constricting, outlets for independent work await you too. In the leisure that Yale students seem to find plenty of and to use in every way besides relaxing, 220 student organizations offer to help you improve the time, in addition to uncounted sports teams, performance groups, social activities, and civic involvements; if you find these offerings too limiting, you surely can — and almost certainly will — found your own avenues for expression or service or commitment. We're aware that, in the friendships you'll build through your life and work together, you will be an education to one another at least as rich as the one we have formally designed. Here again you will be living in an economy of abundance. The group you now join contains people of every known class, race, region, belief, party, appearance, taste, and tradition. Nothing except silly shyness will block your free access to the educations you embody each for the other.

Soon the luxuries of such a world will become habitual to you. Before that happens it would be well to try to realize how very strange the condition is that I have been describing — by which I mean both how unusual the degree of freedom is you will be enjoying and how curious it is, how far from self-evident as a social arrangement, that this experience of enlarged oppor-tunity and relaxed restriction should be set aside for any group, however talented. In some ways it is the detractors of the modern American university who take the most accurate measure of the university's enigmatic liberalities. For some, as you know, the freedom of a school like Yale is a scandal, mere vacuous permissiveness posing in the glory robes of old-fashioned high-mindedness. We, the teachers and administrators of a school that sets so few formal requirements, are taken to exemplify the bankruptcy of the modern professoriate, so morally soft and intellectually vagued-out that we lack the conviction and the nerve to tell students what they ought to know. You are equally caricatured as the student as consumer, a self-indulgent elite set free to pursue its expensive tastes in the mall world of proliferating academic options.

Many academics dismiss these belittling diagnoses as not worthy of reply, but to do so is a mistake. We should face the fact that there would be something highly questionable about the massive freedoms a university affords if they were conducive only to easy learning pleasures. Let's even admit that, placed in thoughtless hands or conjoined to mindless goals, this freedom could result in a pointless accumulation of random agreeable experiences: "liberal education" in the dubious sense of the word. (But here I could paraphrase John Stuart Mill: There would be no difficulty in proving any educational program to work ill, if we suppose universal idiocy to be conjoined with it.) Even if these things were conceded, a university like Yale would think many times before undertaking heavily to regulate the educational experience of its undergraduates—not because these freedoms can't be abused, but because these same freedoms are the precondition for education as we understand and practice it.

Two principles underwrite our requirement of your freedom. First, the university takes the most widely achievable freedom of thought as the essence of its project. For its complete operation a society needs many sorts of institutions: places where things are made; places where things are exchanged; places where things are solemnly believed or idly enjoyed; but it also needs places where things are questioned and reflected on. The reason is that nothing in human grasp is ever yet the whole truth, so that every achieved human understanding looks for its further completion to the process of challenge, amplification, reaffirmation, or revision. The university offers to host this activity of questioning and testing, but to do so it has to strive to keep itself a place of systematically opened minds: a place where nothing is so true that it can't be challenged, and nothing so far out that it can't be entertained for the sake of the under-standing it might yield. Wilhelm von Humboldt, one of the founders of the idea of the modern university, wrote: "It is . . . characteristic of institutions of higher learning that they always treat knowledge as a yet unsolved problem," and again: "Every-thing depends upon holding to the principle of considering knowledge as something not yet found, never completely to be discovered, and searching relentlessly for it as such."

The university sponsors a general freedom of thought for the sake of its intellectual mission; it also offers large powers of choosing as part of the training it extends. Let me return to my imaginary detractor. Looking at a school like this, where students have access to banks on banks of advisors but where little is mandated and the individual is finally responsible for the emerging shape of his or her education, it is easy to imagine a doubter saying: Do you mean to tell me that you let the student know better than the teacher what the student should learn? I think an official reply could only be: (1) The students we bring here have already had abundant and rigorous education, and can't be assumed to be dumb. (2) While they are here they are exposed to the persuasions of many educational points of view, so that the claims of any knowledge to importance won't be lost on them. (3) In this strong-minded and hyperarticulate com-munity they won't lack for people willing to tell them what they think they should know. (4) But at the end of the day, yes, that is just what we do mean to say: here the student makes the choices that design the education. Why: because youth is thought infallible, or because it doesn't really matter what you learn and don't learn? Hardly. You are entrusted with this power in the belief that your thoughtful exploration of alternatives is the essence of education—in the belief that learning is venturing into the space of competing possibilities and doing the difficult work of assessing and choosing among them.

I'm aware that the fine ideas I hold out to you could be reduced to empty platitudes, but I refuse to concede that they need be. But in order for these ideals to have a semblance of reality something is required of you—namely that you work continually to realize the freedom of this place, that you actively extend yourself toward the multiple possibilities that will surround you, actually make choices with some thoughtful sense of the logic of your decisions—and not less that you work to protect the freedom of others. Intellectual freedom is always menaced, not just by the obvious foes I've mentioned but by subtler ones that the very intelligent are by no means immune to. To get the good of this place you'll want to resist the temptation of like-mindedness—the urge to buy acceptance from any group by giving up the right to question what that group believes in. You'll want to resist the pleasures of self-righteousness—the urge to treat others as if nothing that a decent person could conceivably think is lodged in any position except one's own. You'll even want to resist your own habits of chronic, thoughtless successfulness. Students as accomplished as you can't fail to have formed the habit of doing well, which frequently translates as the habit of doing what you think others expect of you in order to make them think you are the kind of person they admire. Compulsive high achievement has carried you far and will carry you farther, but this version of success doesn't count as an ultimate good here. Yale's real successes are not the students who turn this place into a steeplechase of externally fixed expectations and clear each hurdle in good form. They are the people who remember to stop occasionally in our collective frenzy to reflect: What kind of question is it interesting to ask? What kind of person is it good to be? What kind of a life would it be good to live? What kind of a world would it be good to try to build?—and who choose the education that helps them to a fuller answer.

When distinguished visitors arrived at medieval towns, they would be ceremonially welcomed and given what was called the freedom of the city. I think of myself as greeting you, you important arrivers, at the gate of the university you are about to enter. Take its privileges seriously and I know what I can say to conclude. Women and Men of the Class of 1998, I give you the freedom of this place. Enter and enjoy the freedom of this place.

A MORE EXEMPLARY LIFE BEGUN

Freshman Address, September 2, 1995

MR. PRESIDENT, colleagues, parents, I extend a warm welcome on this great occasion. But I reserve my most enthusiastic welcome for you, the Men and Women of the Yale College Class of 1999. A line from Shakespeare that sets the high-water mark in the literature of welcomes says just what I feel on your arrival: you are "welcome hither as is the spring to the earth." All summer we've been waiting for your coming. Everything we know about you tells us that you bring a great surge of vitality to our collective world. So welcome: we rejoice that you have joined us. It is also not lost on me that you are Yale College's last premillennial class, and so that you embody our last chance, for this thousand years, to get things absolutely right. It's a lot to ask of you, perfectly to fulfill the promise of this place, but this is your mission in the next four years. Good luck! I'm optimistic.

This assembly serves a multiple function. It marks your official induction into the world of Yale, now just accomplished. It will also serve as what in your earlier life was called Quiet Time, an officially enforced midafternoon pause designed to let you settle down from the frenzy of exchanging names, trying to find out where (or what) Linsly Chittenden is, deciding how many activities you've never before engaged in you ought to sign up for, and the other joys of new arrival. On our side, this ceremony gives us a chance to see your class drawn up in regimental formation — an impressive spectacle — and to engage in some serious private conversation about what lies ahead. You'll object that a chat with a group of 1,300 is not exactly intimate, but I promise each of you: these words are directed only to you. Forget about the others you see around you, since I have a message for your ears alone.

My message is this. You've come to one of the great fresh starts in your life, one of the few chances your life will offer to step away from the person you've been taken for and decide anew what you would like to become. We busy you so much in these first days that you may be tempted to think that transacting all this business is your goal at Yale. But you are not here, deep down, to discharge our official requirements (though you are certainly not free *not* to). Yale will only open its rewards to you if you meet its expectations with some expectations of your own, if you put our resources in the service of some idea you have defined of what you want your education to give you. James Merrill, the great poet of your now-native state whose death we mourned last winter, speaks of the thought arising in the privacy of night "of a more exemplary life begun / Tomorrow, truer, harder to get right." Far be it from me to say what exemplary life you should propose for yourself, but I implore you not to miss this opportunity to chart one. This is, I know, a taller task than finding the location of the math placement exam.

Far be it from me to delimit what you choose to make of yourself here — far from me to intrude on the privacy of such resolves. But if I were less scrupulous, I know what I would try to insinuate into your idea of your new life. My suggestions arise from the nature of this peculiar entity, the university. The place you have come to is and does a thousand things, but two ideas hold it together. First, this community is unified by a sense of the beauty of excellence in its many forms and the pleasure of striving to attain it. Second, the university is a community of inquiry: that is, a community founded on the premise that nothing is yet the whole of the truth. In saying this the university does not mean that nothing is true, or that there is no such thing as the truth. Rather, it means that no human understanding has or could contain the whole of the truth — that nothing is so true that it is not susceptible to expansion, challenge, revision, and deeper realization.

People sometimes try to bludgeon humanists with the notion that the sciences, the haven of exact measure and objective validation, are the only home of hard knowledge. But when you join in the enterprise of science in this university, you will discover that it has a much livelier sense of the truth: that it is driven by the energizing interplay of theoretical speculation and empirical experiment, not the worship of static objectivity, and that the typical response to a new discovery is not to close up shop but to ask what *else* that discovery would imply, what *other* mystery it might help us address. (Were science not an activity where truth is struggled toward, not thought of as finally achieved, you might be about to study the phlogiston theory of matter.)

People sometimes consider my own field as a preserve of timeless texts embodying the sum of wisdom, and we are right to admire the power humans have shown to *express* their condition, to raise life to self-knowledge through the mirror of art. But literature's greatest admirers recognize that no book can hold the whole of wisdom. Like focusing a camera, the very concentrations that let a work pull some aspect of life into high relief necessarily put other aspects out of the picture, so that we must turn from one book to another, then another, to gain the amassing knowledge no single text could teach.

We have admitted you to this college. But if you want to be admitted to its deep activity, you'll need more than a room assignment and a signed program of courses. You'll need to join in the spirit of this place: you'll need to give up the pretense that you already know the last word about anything and join in the work of education — of collectively struggling toward the improved understanding none of us yet fully possesses. This will require that you accept the serious obligation to be a partner in and giver of education. Both in your formal classes and in the equally educative world of social interactions, you'll need to come forward and share what you know, share it most broadly and generously. Self-withholding shyness, a relatively sympathetic vice in the world at large, is a disaster here, since when you hold back you deprive the rest of us of what you could have taught us. Simultaneously, even as you put yourself forward most actively and confidently, you'll need to remember that you still have things to learn, and so need to open yourself to others' different, even opposite, points of view—and open yourself (this is the hard part) in the sincere belief that they may have something to teach you. Since I became dean I've only heard one line from a student's lips that I found unmitigatedly depressing: "I care so deeply about this issue that I wouldn't even want to know a person who did not agree with me about it." Human, all too human, but profoundly antieducational—since education comes not from hunkering down in well-defended camps of agreement but from facing the challenge of other points of view, and being open to hearing, in them, that part of the truth that one's own point of view has not yet managed to contain.

I'm outlining an approach that will give you the maximum benefit from your four years here. But unkind though it may seem to look even farther ahead ("We just got here!" I hear you wailing), I confess that I'm thinking not just about your college years but about how they might shape your later life in the world. What is a college education for? What does it equip one to do? More than imparting any particular skill or expertise, a school like this aspires to produce what an earlier generation called leaders—by which we mean not just the presidents, premiers, heads of large corporations, Nobel Prize winners, media idols, revolutionizing inventors, famous humanitarians, and other eminences you may or may not become, but good people in the world: people who, in every area of human activity, bring some large measure of energy, imagination, and reflectiveness to the collective enterprise; people who improve the liveliness and thoughtfulness of the collective conversation.

Am I the only one who thinks that the world could use such gifts? You come to college at a time when many issues that had been the subject of widely shared agreement under the post–New Deal and Cold War consensus—what kind of global role this country should aspire to, what size military investment is therefore appropriate, what sort of military action beyond our shores that role requires; what levels of inequality are tolerable within this society, what obligations the well off have to the ill off, what changes in social practice the state should require to help realize the dream of equal opportunity—these questions and others equally profound have come wide open in your early adulthood, and as they move toward new resolution this should be a time of great debate. But debate in any very rich sense is just what we do not have much of at this time. Our public conversation largely takes the form of pushing the buttons that activate passionate convictions, preconceptions that themselves stay unexamined and undefended and that seek to crush opposition with contempt rather than reason with it. What do we need? "We need CHANGE," I've been told by contemporaries liberal, conservative, and maverick. But if we stop and ask which exact changes we need, and how we can be sure those changes will make the difference we seek, and how we can keep today's reforms from generating tomorrow's problems, you know the answer: "He just doesn't get it."

What is not so much in evidence, but what we're going to need if we're not going to lurch from one ill-considered change to another, is some shared recognition that the great questions of our time are not easy to be absolutely right about and require hard collective thought. We will need as well a more sincere effort to enter into conversation with those who don't already agree with us and to convince them by making them feel the force of better arguments—an art that requires imagining what someone else's position looks like from the inside. Together with more authentic effort at persuasion, the sort of debate that will lead to thoughtful choices will require improvement in the arts of listening—of making ourselves open to others' potential wisdom even as we subject them to our own.

Your work here will be highly relevant to our society's needs as I've described them. Rightly engaged, this school will be a daily practice ground for your powers of complex reflection and mutually enlightening exchange—powers you can then take out into the world. But let's not assume that you will mystically receive these benefits just by enrolling here. To develop these powers, you'll need to want them and you'll need to work for them. This means that you'll need to set them as goals, not just in moderately inspiring ceremonial moments, but in the grind of every day, when the desires to be right and to regard those not so minded as a lower form of life rise up to waylay you. You'll face these enemies, as all mortals do. But it will help if you think of them as something to fight against, not as sources of pride or proofs of your virtue.

"A more exemplary life begun / Tomorrow, truer, harder to get right." It's a lot to ask, and I've had some fear that my talk may appall you with its strenuous expectations. But nothing we know about you suggests that you would enjoy anything much easier. We have chosen you, after all, on the basis of your proven eagerness to take on hard tasks and work to get them right. So let me bid you to this pleasurable challenge in the years we'll spend together. Try to make it your business to be an educated person—a person whose education is never over, a person still engaged in the exchange through which understanding is moved toward.

2000 AND YOU

Freshman Address, August 31, 1996

MR. PRESIDENT, colleagues, families, and friends, please join me in welcoming the Yale College Class of 2000. Men and Women of the Class of 2000, I rejoice to greet you, and to administer the mystic gestures that admit you to citizenship in Yale College. I'm told that in some places this occasion is used to inspire new recruits with the all-but-incapacitating rigor of the ordeal that lies ahead. "Look to the right; look to the left," the designated authoritarian is supposed to say; "the program you're entering is so strenuous that only one of every two of you will make it through alive." I've always wanted to try that line, but honesty compels me to admit that Yale expects for you to succeed here, not to fail. You'll find plenty of rigor, but you've shown yourselves to be people who delight in the demanding and in your power to meet it. So at the risk of disappointing the masochists among you, I can only say at your initiation: Look to the left; look to the right. You are now in the company of talented people. Rejoice in one another's gifts and in the opportunities you'll seize together. I know that you will flourish.

There is a subject that I seem doomed to take up with you, much though I would like to avoid it. I refer to the astonishing date of your expected graduation. The impending arrival of the 21st century has already become such a cliche that one reason to look forward to it is that people will stop exhorting us toward it. No longer will we be asked to seek leadership for the 21st century, or telecommunications for the 21st century, or vinyl siding for the 21st century, or other nostrums that come clothed in this appeal. Still, even such a cliche-averse person as myself has to admit that the Class of 2000 has a certain ring to it. Chance facts (the year you happened to be born) and unremarkable procedures (our habit of designating classes by the year of their expected completion) have joined to lift your class into the category of the extraordinary. Nineteen ninety-six is just another four-digit number; 2000 is emphatically not.

Let's recall why this is so. First, 2000 partakes of that sense of occult significance that has always attached to numbers and their mysterious regularities. I remember in my distant childhood sitting in the hot back seat of my family's car during endless drives toward distant vacations, then becoming riveted by the discovery that the odometer was at some mileage like 59,998.4, or 79,999.2. Boredom turned at once to fascination: we were on the verge of a mega-turnover! In a few short minutes I would get to watch five digits turn simultaneously and one number sign fill five adjacent columns! (Now you know how I spent my youth.) The year you graduate will possess this potent aura of the mathematical occult, its three consecutive zeroes promising not another year but some huge new beginning, its weird and insistent repetitions – 0, 0, 0 – seeming the work of no mere chance or mundane arithmetic but of a hidden providential hand.

Compounding this effect, the year 2000 will also put a new digit in the thousand column, and so will activate profound cultural expectations attached to the idea of the millennium. In a religious tradition going back 2,000 years – Revelations 20 is its major biblical articulation, though the idea has antecedents in ancient Zoroastrianism – the millennium is the time when this world, seemingly so final, will be abolished, replaced by a world freed from Satan's power where redeemed souls will reign with the messiah for a thousand years. Belief in the millennium has a particularly intense tradition in this country. When Father William Miller calculated that the world would end between March 1843 and March 1844, one historian tells us, "well over fifty thousand people in the United States became convinced that time would run out in 1844, while a million or more of their fellows were skeptically expectant." So intense were the expectations of Miller's followers that some donned glory robes and gathered on high places to be ready for their ascent into heaven, and others refused to plant or harvest crops in 1844, since this world would soon be no more. Among their other accomplishments, graduates of your college have made major contributions to American millenarian history. Timothy Dwight, now a residential college but once a Yale President, made millennial calculations in his spare time. John Humphrey Noyes, the founder of 19th-century America's most elegant utopian community, came to his vision of millennial perfectionism while a student at Yale. Jonathan Spence has found that a Yale College graduate, the missionary Edward Stevens, gave Hong Xiuquan the religious materials that sparked his millenarian and messianic visions, visions that fueled the Taiping Rebellion in mid-19th-century China.

I have no doubt that millennial expectation will break out with increasing virulence in even the most secular parts of our culture as we approach the year 2000, unleashing waves of hope, dread, and strange behavior. This anticipation is what seems to mark you, vaguely uncanny Class of 2000, with an air of special promise or special destiny. I know this feeling; I share it to some extent; but I doubt that the coming calendar shift will do all that we expect. When I watched the odometer in my overheated youth, I would often forget and look away when the zeroes all came up, but when, by practicing a strict attentiveness, I would see the numbers actually shift, would catch the magic moment in the very act of occurring, I would learn that nothing very thrilling attended this change—that mile 50,000 proved one more number in a rising numerical sequence, not a transcendence of that sequence. Father Miller's followers got ready for the end of the world, and when it failed to happen they recalculated the date and got ready again, but when the millennial moment came and passed, it had not brought the redeemed new order. "Still in the cold world," one Millerite wrote with awful pathos the day after the appointed change. Though I may be proved wrong, I am expecting the year 2000 to prove a thumping anticlimax—a year pretty much like any other. So while I'm tempted to elate you with the rhetoric of your special promise, it seems more prudent to guess that when you leave here it will be to enter not a brave new world but a new phase of our same old world: a world just as constricting and just as rich in possibility, just as resistant and just as susceptible to human creativity, as the one we now know.

As a wise counsellor looking out for your future, then, I want to advise you: do plant your fields; do harvest your crops; enjoy your millennial associations, but don't be taken in by them. But since none of us will escape the force of these expectations, I propose this revision of my counsel. The approach of the millennium has always inspired an urgent desire to use the short interval that remains to get ready, to be prepared. My premillennial counsel to you is: don't expect to be done with this world anytime soon; but do keep alive the sense that you are headed toward a critical future; and use this sense to help make your Yale years a serious season of preparation.

What are you going to be after college? What are you going to want to do in the world for which your time here could help equip you? Please do not mistake me to be asking what future job you're heading for—a rude question on this occasion and by no means a sufficient guide to how your education should be shaped. In a world so fraught with transformation as ours, you will need the skills to seize the multiple, continually emerging and currently unforeseeable opportunities that a changing world will put before you. Those who prepare too narrowly now are likely to find themselves prepared, in time, for a career that no longer exists. In any case, I trust that even the most jobocentric of you will want to have a life, in which case you'll want to be prepared for other things in addition to your career.

I've asked myself what would be a comprehensive enough name for the preparation you could seek here and my summer reading has supplied an answer. In Richmond Lattimore's translation of *The Odyssey* the hero is called with magnificent iteration "resourceful Odysseus." When I ask myself what will you need to be, in order to be continuingly effective in a changing world, I light with pleasure on this word "resourceful." It carries at least these meanings: (1) capable of generating sources of interest and action from within; (2) mentally well-furnished, equipped with knowledge won from wide experience, and able to use stored understandings to meet new situations; (3) "capable of devising ways and means" — the good dictionary definition; one who embraces situations as challenges to his or her ingenuity, not immutable dooms, an active contriver of ways to avert the worst and to find opportunities where none are apparent.

Isn't this what you would wish to become — Resourceful . . . add your own name? I can hardly believe that you want to be the opposite of resourceful: inert, inept, helpless, clueless. And if you agree that you'd like to be resourceful eventually, wouldn't this be the time to begin building your resources? You could be doing so every day you're here if you seek all occasions to multiply and fortify your powers — and if you resist all temptations to incomplete development.

In particular, let me beg you not to let your addiction to being good at things confine you to the things you're already good at — a sure route to self-limitation. I have heard of students who, having simulated daunting skills at certain subjects while applying here, upon arrival suddenly decide that they have all along been afflicted with a profound inability in that area, and so should be excused from further contact. But the joys of exemption would be less appealing to you if you took yourself seriously as a candidate for resourcefulness. You live at a time when the origin of the universe is becoming available for more precise dating and viewing; when new information technologies annually transform the nature of information; when genetic processes wholly mysterious a short while ago have become so well understood that genetic alteration is a growing possibility. In face of such developments, whether you "like" science hardly seems the right question. Would you really be willing to have these dimensions of reality remain forever opaque to you when they could lie open to your powers of mind? On the other hand, who will best help us think through the moral quandaries that will be raised by genetic engineering: someone trained only in science, or one who has also had some exercise in ethical reflection? Living as you will in a global society, where events at any one point are determined by multiple developments in regions spatially remote, will you really be competent to your world if you don't learn multiple languages — and also the cultural histories that give world-integrating forces their very different local spins?

And as we speak of a global future, let's not pretend that nearer problems now hold no further interest. Nineteen ninety-six is the 100th anniversary of the Supreme Court decision that legitimated racial segregation in American schools. Our country has again grown tired of caring about problems of inequality and social division, but it's unlikely that irritable dismissal of these problems will rid us of their consequences. We must hope that some of you will craft new approaches to such issues that can achieve a new social persuasiveness. But if you're going to have good ideas about these problems later, wouldn't it help to start thinking about them now?

I don't intend to list every power that you could develop. I only want to remind you that your enablement, the richer or thinner development of your powers, is at stake in what you choose to do here. Your new home is endowed with magnificent resources to support the work of self-development — massive collections; a distinguished faculty; lively and talented classmates best of all. But living in proximity to resources can't be expected to make you resourceful. For that you'll need to engage the opportunities that surround you. Yale will only build your strengths to the extent that you exercise yourself upon its facilities.

Women and men of Yale's newest class, we won't all meet together again until the next time you gather en masse on this spot, at your graduation. By then it will be 2000, which may or may not prove a year of wonders. But we'll have wonders enough to celebrate if you take my advice. Engage yourself in the life of this place, seize all occasions to test out your powers, and on that great day I'll be able to say: Look to the left; look to the right; admire with me this company of resourceful people. I might confer an even better Homeric epithet upon you. Robert Fitzgerald, a freer translator than Lattimore and a greater poet, has Homer call Odysseus "that man skilled in all ways of contending." Men and women skilled in all ways of contending: that could be you! And will be, if you use this place in the right spirit.

WHAT IS FITTING

Freshman Address, August 30, 1997

WHAT AN ASTONISHING coincidence! My friends and I have set out for a stroll, and who should we run into but the Yale College Class of 2001! By yet more amazing chance, we had decided to try out our academic casualwear, and you too have gone in for an elegant formality! What could this massive fashion statement mean? We have put on non-customary outfits to mark an extra-ordinary occasion: the start of a great new life. Think of it. You are released forever from the stressful and absorbing work of getting into college. No more standardized testing for you, no more essays requiring you to explain, with becoming modesty, why you are the most impressive person you've ever known. More seriously, you are crossing the threshold into a space of wildly enriched possibility, a world where opportunities for discovery and self-discovery will assault you at every turn. And since you have reached the age of reason, the restrictions needful for the immature will now be very largely suspended, so that you will confront these opportunities with expanded freedom and responsibility. On this occasion, when I name the new school you have come to, I mean to indicate the new chances and powers you've come for. You will now understand me when I say (when I say it it's official, so prepare yourself for a life-altering pronouncement): Men and Women of the Class of 2001, welcome to Yale College.

Two thousand one is a resonant number here even without its futuristic associations. Yale College having been founded in 1701, you have the distinction of being Yale's tercentennial class, and we will celebrate Yale's 300th birthday together with your graduation. This fact could remind you that in entering Yale you are stepping into a long-running history. When the personal computer was born, Yale was already 280 years old. When electric power was first commercially available and telephone networks first established, Yale was already nearly 180. The Civil War and the Emancipation Proclamation are nearer to the present than they are to Yale's beginning. To go back to the great early landmark of the American women's movement, the Seneca Falls Convention of 1848, is to cross just half the distance between 1997 and 1701. Among more venerable rivals, Yale is older than the American nation and modern democratic government; older than the industrial revolution; older than modern capitalism, Adam Smith's *The Wealth of Nations* having appeared so recently as 1776.

What you are coming into has been going on for a long time. But when people come here as students, whoever Yale may have belonged to before, it becomes their place—theirs to enjoy and theirs to help create. I wonder if you have any idea how much Yale is about to be in your power. Every year when we admit a class, we put this place at risk. The joyous creativity of students here, their high-spirited pursuit of excellence in a thousand forms of work and play, helps make the supremely interesting world that Yale-lovers love. But what if some year Yale fell into the hands of dullards and lethargiacs? This whole place could go dead. In the discussion classes that are so common here each student has the power to help co-create a deepening group awareness, to join the inquiry and lead it to unexpected turns. If some year students fell into docility or torpor, just wanted to be told the answer and go back to bed, there would be a stiff price for us: the whole activity of understanding would have been diminished. This is now your place, and it is now for you to give it life and realize its promise. My first message to you was a joyful welcome, but I follow it with a stern command: Now get to work; make this place happen.

But what is it that happens here? Let me approach an answer by going back in history. In the 17th century New Eng-

land was settled by religious dissidents whose brand of Protes-
tantism attached crucial importance to the idea of a learned
clergy. For this reason, these immigrants had already established
a college in New England (Harvard; you may have heard of it)
within six years of their settlement at Boston. By 1700 colonists
who had pushed on from Massachusetts to Connecticut had
formed the idea of founding a college of their own, to save the
expense and difficulty of travel to then-distant Cambridge but
also to rescue education from the spiritual morass Harvard was
thought to have descended into, that school being judged to
have become a scene of "riot and pride, profuseness and prodi-
gality" and creeping open-mindedness on religious issues.

The early history of this new college is a record of fragile
survival among almost unimaginable vicissitudes. I have
known day care centers that were institutionally much more
formidably established than Yale in its first 30 years. Were time
not short I would tell you how the Collegiate School of Connecticut (as it was first called) met in the home of a teacher with
another full-time job as pastor, in a settlement so remote that
the 13 students threatened not to stay; how, having lost its first
rector, this school limped along without a leader for more than a
decade; how in this time dissension among Yale's sponsors
became so aggravated that its trustees allowed its minuscule
operation to break up into three separate fragments, one meeting in Wethersfield, one in New Haven, and one in Saybrook;
how, once it was decided to regather the school in New Haven,
the custodian of the Saybrook operation refused to send along
the school's only asset, a library, which then had to be seized by
sheriffs and forcibly transported.

The school so founded was a place for training and the
transmission of knowledge, with both governed by a strong
belief in the rightness of an established order. The earliest Yale
was organized to prepare young men for relatively fixed social
roles in a fixed social hierarchy. What the founders called "perpetuating the Christian Protestant Religion, by a succession of
Learned and Orthodox men" — replicating the congregational
ministry, the role of highest professional status and spiritual

authority in this culture — was at the center of this school's mission, though Yale did open its sights more broadly. (An early document speaks of the intention to found a school "wherein Youth . . . may be fitted for Publick employment both in Church and Civil State.") Yale further showed its loyalty to a fixed order through the custom (preserved through the 1760s) of "ranking" its student body — that is, compelling them to sit in assigned places mirroring the hierarchical order of their parent's social stations.

This oldest Yale was hardly interested in free thinking. It meant to teach what was true and right to know (note that Yale's founders use "Learned" and "Orthodox" as parallel adjectives), and it mandated respect for authority through a thousand daily practices. It will interest you to learn that when your 18th-century predecessors entered Yale, they wrote out a copy of the college regulations as a sign of their acceptance. In 1741 the Yale College faculty voted that students who called the President or faculty members Hypocrites should be punished on the first offense by public confession, and on the second by expulsion. My favorite ancient regulation suggests a fear virtually of undergraduate speech itself, ruling that "All students shall be slow to speak and avoid . . . profane swearing, lying, needless asseverations, foolish garrulings, chidings, strifes, railings, gesting, uncomely noise, spreading ill rumor, divulging secrets, and all manner of troublesome and offensive behavior."

I call up this distant original to help mark some features of this place today. Let me note some striking contrasts. Modern Yale is not very interested in your ascribed or inherited attributes. We seek and will continue to seek students of ability from every social origin; but wherever you come from, please do not expect others to be unduly impressed by that fact. Who you are at Yale will be a function of what you make of yourself here, not who you or your family were back home. Second, contemporary Yale is and long has been a secular institution, a place that gives equal welcome to all sincere convictions and enforces no one belief. So far from aiming at the transmission of orthodoxy, this is now a place of the open question, a place that exists for exploration and the testing of received ideas. Third, and just for this reason, Yale now not only tolerates but actively requires your speech, putting up even with your needless asseverations and foolish garrulings to create a space for your fresh thinking and sincere inquiring.

So different is this school from what its founders had in mind that they would probably recoil from it in horror. But if they could master their outrage and dismay, they might recognize a deeper continuity; for in a broad interpretation of the phrase we are still in the business of "fitting youth for Publick employment in Church and Civil State." Yale still seeks students with the promise to be social leaders — by which we mean not just the people who will monopolize the prestige, make the big money, and boss people around, but men and women who in every activity, in every community, will bring some large measure of imagination, dynamism, and thoughtfulness to the collective life.

Yale is here to help "fit" you for "publick employment" in this expansive sense; but let me pause a little over this interesting word "fit." In one of its meanings, "fit" describes the extent to which one thing approximates the size and shape of another, and the process by which it is made to conform to that size and shape. Those nice clothes fit you; if they didn't, you went into the fitting room to have them fitted. I can't accept the idea that you have come here to be fitted in this sense. I hope you will not leave here unfit, but it would be quite uninspiring to think that you had come here to be snipped at and restitched, sawed, planed, and sanded, the more smoothly to slip into the existing array of worldly careers. You will have a job, no doubt you will even excel at it, but your life will require more of you than being securely employed: it will require you to rise to the now-unforeseeable challenges and to grasp the as-yet-unimaginable opportunities that your world will confront you with. In her new book on the Declaration of Independence, Pauline Maier cites Thomas Jefferson writing late in life to John Adams: "It was the lot of our early years to witness nothing but the dull monotony of colonial subservience, and of riper ones to breast the labors and perils of working out of it." Who can say what crises or chances you'll be the one to face? But in whatever history awaits you, you will want to be able to be an actor, someone who helps face the problems and contrive the solutions. This is what makes me think that if Yale's work is the work of fitting, it must be fitting in another sense. "Fitting" also means "to put in a condition of readiness," and "fit" means strong, ready, able to bring one's powers to bear because those powers have been well trained.

As you enter it, I urge you to think of Yale as a giant fitness center in this sense of the word. What you can do here is to build your strengths: the stored knowledge, the powers of analysis and articulation, the disciplined creativity, the habits of communal involvement that will let you be effective in your world. You should think of Yale's multitudinous resources and activities as the exercise apparatus that could make you fit. Maybe you've seen those machines with signs affixed saying how they are to be used and which muscles they build. To get the good of them, you should compose such signs for the resources now around you. Do so and you'll see each of your potential courses in terms of the corner of reality it could open up for you and the powers of analysis it could develop; a much better ground for choosing classes than whether they have an allegedly cool teacher or meet at a convenient hour. Heed my advice and you won't approach your new classmates by just seeking out the compatible and shunning the annoying. You'll understand each of them, exactly to the extent that they are not like you, as embodying an aspect of experience previously closed to you, a knowledge their friendship could open up. Your residential college and your new city could be just your new backdrop, a place for you to live in. But if you looked at them as strength-builders you'd see them as places to exercise your powers of citizenship, the skills of living together so as to improve each private lot. The debates that will enliven this campus could give you the chance to air preprogrammed attitudes; or they could be your chance to enter into hard issues and fathom their complexities, the better to work out solutions not now in sight.

Women and Men of the Class of 2001: I have no trouble imagining that when you go forth from here as Yale's 300th class, you will be magnificently capable, ready for anything. This place opens itself to you to assist you toward this goal. But please remember the oldest lesson of fitness centers: you don't get their benefit by taking out a membership and paying the dues. You have to work out there, to exert yourself with strenuous energy: this place will build your strengths just in the measure that you engage it with your full powers. Mark Twain said that he never recognized an opportunity until it has ceased to be one, but this need not be your fate. Enter into this place, exercise yourself freely and vigorously, engage its challenges with your most generous energy, and you'll be fit enough for what lies beyond. If you don't, I'll have a fit.

THE WAY TO WORRY

Freshman Address, August 29, 1998

MR. PRESIDENT, colleagues, parents, suspiciously well-dressed men and women sitting here before me: I am concerned because we have detected a defect in your college entrance. Here you are, already very successfully impersonating Yale students, indeed already acting as if you own the place. But I know you know, deep down, that you have failed to have the experience of officially entering Yale. You were admitted here, a fairly official act, but college was then still far ahead of you. All summer you have received our mailings, but as it drew nearer Yale was still at a distance. You have now arrived on campus, but you surely have not mistaken the combination summer camp, schmooze marathon, recruitment drive, and low-grade furniture mart you have seen so far for the real Yale. Soon classes will have started, but then you'll be too busy to watch for the moment of your official debut. So it is that the exact moment of your entry into Yale will at first seem to lie before you, then somehow already behind you, without having ever actually taken place.

If this has caused you worry, I hasten to bring relief. The purpose of this gathering is to mark some moment as the exact time when you became students of Yale College. Let's say that time is now. Men and Women of the Class of 2002, welcome to Yale College.

Your time here, which will include both the millennium and Yale's 300th birthday, should be exciting enough. But excitement sometimes brings anxiety in its train; and it occurs to me that, under your show of composure, you may have come with hidden apprehensions. I want to speak to these apprehensions, and having already lifted one massive burden from your minds, I will now direct my therapeutic powers to another.

In my current position, I have been approached by Yale graduates 10, 20, 30, even 50 years out who have wanted to confess to the Dean some undetected college sin that has gnawed at them for years. (I'm not making this up.) Though there is some variety in the list of hoarded iniquities, by far the most frequent confession I receive is this: "I wanted to tell you that I have always believed that I was admitted to Yale by mistake." "I, I alone among my Yale classmates, was there as a fraud," a more elaborate version runs; "while every one of my contemporaries was obviously qualified, I alone was secretly dubious." Varying specifics can then be added to the main body of this confession, as for instance: "I knew I was an impostor because I was really not the supernaturally gifted being my application essay had described." Further variants are then produced by taking any distinctive feature of oneself and construing it as a deficiency. "I probably just got in because I came from the area," I have heard; but also: "I probably just got in because I came from a remote area." Or again: "I went to a school with a lot of advantages, and I was probably admitted on the strength of those advantages, not my own attributes"; but also: "I went to a school with no advantages; I could never have been the equal of those people who went to really good schools." "I was just an athlete"; "I was just an intellectual"; "I was just well-connected"; "they took me to have an outsider": such confessions have taught me that the one talent humans share is the talent for feeling insufficient, then believing their insufficiency is their unique possession.

Yale College Class of 2002, you look immensely self-assured. But my experience teaches that, 20 years from now, some future dean may be receiving confessions of this sort from any number of you. So if there are any present who share this fantasy in any form or to any extent, I bring you a message on the highest authority. If you have felt the slightest doubt about your presence here, I want to say to you: (1) I am appalled at your lack of originality. The real secret about this shameful secret is that it's an overwhelmingly common experience, as you'd learn if you were a little more candid with one another. (2) What low opinion do you have of your university, what level of incompetence do you attribute to us, that we would admit 1,300 students each by a separate act of mistake? As for the truth-inflation in your personal statement, rest assured: we had suspected it already. (3) You are in fact the very person we wanted to come here, the one we chose in place of many others. But further: (4) Yale doesn't want students who are acceptable in the sense of barely clearing some fixed bar or minimally meeting some fixed criterion. We seek students endowed with the whole range of human gifts who share the drive to develop their gifts to the fullest extent, for their own pleasure and for the good of others; and we count on our students not just to be adequate to the demands of this place but to enrich its life, to help make it happen. When I welcome you to the Yale community, I mean that Yale welcomes the talents and energies you bring here, confident they will help you get the good of this place and enrich its collective life.

If you are nervous on entering Yale, please remember that the strength of anxiety is no proof of its accuracy as a diviner of future truth. To worry is just human: Those of you interested in artificial intelligence will know you have simulated the human mind when you can make machines capable of sickening themselves with worry for no discernible cause. Anxiety arises especially in transitions to new situations — and you are now making one of the great threshold crossings life has in store: a crossing not just into college but into the freedoms of full adulthood.

So what follows if you are occasionally daunted? That you should have stayed home? That you should go back to high school? While I would think you truly peculiar if you could enter Yale with absolutely no apprehension, I can't believe that you have no taste for a challenge. Anxiety is the negative experience of the mental energy released by unfamiliar situations. In other words, anxiety is the experience in negative form of the same energy that is positively experienced as excitement. That said, it cannot be my mission to wish to cure or relieve you of all disquiet. My mission is to urge you to embrace the nervous energy unleashed by a new beginning and convert it to positive form: the form that will make you seek, not flee, the challenge of your new life.

With this for a prelude, let me coach you in some right and wrong ways to worry. There are probably people in this room who have felt intermittent concern about whether they will do well at Yale. I assure you, we want and we expect you to succeed here. But what do you want me to tell you: that nothing will be a struggle? That as a kindness to you, we have been careful to admit only people who are your certifiable inferiors? Discovering new powers through the exercise of your strengths in the company of talented people will be the joy of your new life, if you remember not to regard it as an intimidation.

While failure is the obvious thing to fear, the reality is that you have far more to fear from your addiction to success. The desire to do well is made by combining authentic love of excellence with the desire to be thought well of by others — an alloy far inferior in value. I worry that your desire to be thought a success might tempt you to try only those things at Yale at which you are already confident of succeeding: a recipe, if not exactly for failure, then certainly for a very limited success. You are coming up to a moment when everything you have ever studied can be engaged at a more challenging and more interesting level and where a hundred things you never had the chance to study will be clamoring for your attention. If you approach this as a chance to do everything you're agreed to be good at and skip everything at which you might possibly be (as we now say) "challenged," the advantages to your record — easily exaggerated — will be hugely outweighed by the cost to your education. Are you confident there is any subject you'll be content to be ignorant of for the rest of your life? I promise you that no one will say of you when you are 40: "He is strangely ignorant, but I hear he got good grades at Yale."

I would make the same plea about your new social environment. It's scary to enter a world of strangers, and I don't suppose that we ever fully overcome the extraordinarily primitive reactions this state touches off: dread of exposure to unknown and possibly hostile glances, the deep urge to build some little personal world to shield us from threatening anonymity. As a once-shy person, I will never underestimate the power of these forces. But just for that reason, I implore you not to let anxiety turn your social life into a social self-enclosure. At a school like this, it is not a platitude to say that your classmates will be among your great teachers. We bring together intelligent and articulate people from different places, with different interests, who know different things and see things in different lights, so that each of you will have access, all day long, to a multiform presentation of what lies outside your current understanding. In consequence, at Yale, the normal processes of daily life will be perpetually subjecting your ways of thinking to other ways, and will give you the continual chance to learn the limits of what you know, to incorporate from others what you find lacking in yourself, and to win a deeper grasp of what you do know and how you know it. Reducing the stress of social encounter in a place like this is not the good thing it might seem. To the extent that you shut yourself in from the whole community, you will deprive yourself of the testing and enrichment that others could have given you — and deprive them of the education you could have given them in return.

Now let me say what is really on my mind. I have known students, upon arriving at Yale, to have worried about the most astonishing range of things, from the relatively humdrum phobias (will the clothes that looked great at home look weird here?) to worries that are more specialized but still not radically strange (will I die if it snows?) to ones that have given me new admiration for the inventive powers of the human mind. (A student from Texas confessed to me that before he got to Yale, he had the fear that all people in the East were very tall.) I can sympathize with every one — almost — of these anxieties. But I have rarely met a student who thought to worry about the one thing that would strike me as really worth worrying about at this point in your career: coming up with some answer to the questions, What is an education and how am I to get one?

I'll tell you what I know. Your education is not only the courses you enroll in, though they form a part of it. Your education is the ongoing process, fed in a hundred ways and never to be completed, by which you win the ability to understand the world in its multitudinous dimensions and to act in the world in a reflective, constructive way. My thinking on this matter has been haunted by a line I found in a letter from Thomas Jefferson to John Adams. Adams and Jefferson were the central figures in the drafting and enacting of the American Declaration of Independence. By uncanny coincidence, they also both died on the 50th anniversary of the signing of the Declaration, July 4, 1826. In the winter of their last year, Jefferson wrote Adams this summary of their early careers: "It was the lot of our early years to witness nothing but the dull monotony of colonial subservience, and of riper ones to breast the labors and perils of working out of it." When we were young, Jefferson declares, we saw nothing around us but a stultifying world whose limitations seemed inescapable. But great changes did await us, and when history brought unforeseen possibilities toward us, we, who had been witnesses or spectators of a dull history, became instead historical actors, performers of the labors and averters of the dangers through which a new nation was created.

How were they able to exert these powers? Not through raw talent alone. Jefferson could draft the Declaration in 1776 because he had mastered a compelling prose style at an earlier age and because he had read as a student—no doubt on a day when it seemed mere homework—the Declaration of Rights of 1689, which supplied the outline for his Declaration. In other words, he could perform the work of civic creativity at a later moment because he had done the work of education at an earlier moment—without having the slightest idea how it might serve him later on.

The world you have known has been strangely immune to the crises that have dominated other parts of this century. But I have no doubt that you will live to face realities more challenging than high consumer confidence and low unemployment. Not for me to guess what the dramas of your time will be. But whatever they are, to face them we will need people who can help seize the opportunity and avert the danger. The people who will be able to act imaginatively and effectively then will be people who funded their minds well now—which leads me back to you.

We didn't accept you because you got good grades and racked up long lists of accomplishments in high school. Nor have we brought you here to perform those feats again. We picked you because we judged you to have the aptitude to lead a thoughtful and constructive life; and we brought you here to help you prepare your powers. But Yale can only do so much. We can offer you opportunities, and we can set minimum requirements for your use of them, but it falls to you to make an education of your time here. You will advance on this goal if you seek out every new domain of knowledge and every challenge that can be posed to your achieved understanding—if you stay, that is, a little adventurous.

Women and men of the Yale College Class of 2002, since you only became Yale students 15 minutes ago, I have the honor to be your first Yale instructor. And behold! After only 15 minutes, you have advanced this far in wisdom. You have learned that anxiety is excitement traveling under a false name, and that the right use of anxiety is not to relieve it but to rechannel it: to use it to fuel the embrace of challenges, not the flight from them. Now that you have learned the right way to worry, I have no further worries on your behalf. I see you here this day on the brink of a great new chapter of your education, which is to say, your life. I know that you will let no part of this opportunity escape you. On behalf of Yale College, I salute you and I cheer you on.

HAZARDS OF SUCCESS

Freshman Address, August 28, 1999

MR. PRESIDENT, colleagues, proud parents, and families, I welcome you to this great ceremony of renewal. Men and Women of the Yale College Class of 2003, I welcome you to your new home. Your arrival is cause for jubilation. Yale is supremely rich in educational resources, but Yale has annual need of people like you to actuate its promise. If we rejoice at the sight of you, it is because your high-spirited creativity and intelligence are the catalysts we need to make the reaction work. If you yourselves should feel some mild joy at this moment, well, who could blame you? I have played board games in which you sometimes have to go back and retrace a stretch you had already traveled, but this will not happen here. Your entry into Yale College means that you are done with high school forever. More amazing still, now that you are in college you will never, ever have to get into college again. All summer long this campus has been crawling with touring family parties, the older members trying not to look too anxiously protective, the younger giving off signals that they scarcely know these older people and are only letting them walk with them to be nice. Within days you will have ceased to think of these creatures as anyone you ever had anything in common with, and will look with kindly condescension at those in the strange if touching plight of needing to look at colleges. There will be no more SATs for you, no more achievement tests, no more essays in which subtly to convey the thought that you might be the most remarkable person your town, state, or nation has ever produced. You have been there; you have done that.

And the consequence is that you are here: entering Yale, crossing the threshold to a great new chapter of your life.

I have known students upon arrival to make the amazing discovery that, in their preoccupation with getting into college, they had given virtually no thought to what one went to college for. If you should suffer from this deficiency, I doubt that your first hours at Yale will have helped you much. You'll have had time to be recruited by various student organizations, time to study novel forms of furniture, time to introduce yourself to perhaps two hundred classmates who now know certain fascinating and revealing things about you (like where you're from), but you have probably not had time to think. Since you are obviously far too busy, in my kindness I have decided to do this job for you. Allow me to think what your reason for coming here might be.

We will require many things of you during the next four years, and you will no doubt impose yet further requirements on yourselves, but at bottom you have only two things to accomplish at Yale. First, you need to use this place to get outside your own head. We all begin our careers in some little world of familiar things and understandings. Education is the process by which we break these barriers to seize a fuller knowledge of the world. You didn't begin this self-enlargement just now and you will not complete it in four years, but at the time when you are newly arrived at the fullness of your powers, Yale is here to help you make this reach of understanding in an intensified way. If you use this place right, you'll learn to see questions where others might see mere givens and will build a richer sense, if not of the answers, then at least of how you might go about developing an answer. When you leave here, our hope is that you will have a mind sufficiently stored and trained to be able to engage the world your experience presents you with in a knowing and constructive fashion; but this is only half of your task. You are also here, through your engagement with a host of challenges, to win a fuller knowledge of your own powers: to learn the range of strengths you can bring to the world and use to make your personal contribution.

Grasping the world in an ever-broadening way, learning what you have to offer as a citizen and shaper of the world—these are the great projects you came to work at. Now, what could block you from advancing on these goals? It's not unlikely that you have brought along with you some intermittent dread that you will not do well here. These fantasies are a predictable product of the moment of arrival, but if you fancy that your personal insecurities are better justified than other people's, I'm sorry to tell you that you're almost certainly wrong. If you have fears of insufficiency, failure, or impending collegiate doom, I hasten to assure you that whatever shocks the first weeks of college may bring you—and I hope you'll find this place at least a little different from the worlds you've already mastered—you are up to it, you will do fine here, you'll manage and probably even flourish.

Nevertheless, you do show one tendency that causes me some fear on your behalf, and I'll name it even if I cause you pain. When I ask myself what might keep you from winning the full measure of what Yale could afford, I see one answer in your habit of chronic high achievement, your incorrigible addiction to success.

We know about your success habit. The shelves of our admissions office groan with the chronicles of your accomplishments. Even with some suitable markdown for inflation, it is clear that you are people of ability who have felt a serious obligation to turn your talents to good account. This sense of obligation no doubt reflects an authentic inward virtue, but I suspect that in each of you it has been amplified at least in some measure by a contributing external force, what I might call the culture of juvenile overachievement. The *New York Times* ran an article this summer about parents who had begun hiring personal batting coaches for their Little League–aged children at $70 an hour to help straighten out their swings. My reaction to this news was complex. On the one hand, I saw the happy prospect that if your career plans should fall through someday, people as talented as you might be able to live lives of affluence and high demand as correctors of the minor flaws of other people's children. As for the child who was tutored, I would be happy if I believed this training boost would turn him into a future Sammy Sosa, but it seems far more likely that what will be raised is not his batting average but his anxiety level, the pressure he will feel to do well in a game made more than ever a scene of triumph or humiliating self-exposure.

But as a student of cultural history, I confess that the principal thought this story provoked was that it marked a new turn in a comparatively recent historical development. It has not long been the case that children of above-average ability were expected to demonstrate that ability on a compulsive basis in every domain of their life. Mozart and Einstein were recognized as prodigies and given opportunities befitting a prodigy, but in their day children who were not prodigies were not expected to perform like ones, and even prodigies were allowed to be incompetent at activities at which they did not shine. (Herr Einstein hired no baseball tutor.) It is only since the 1950s, and in the accelerated form we now know it is only really since the middle 1980s, that it has ever seemed plausible to expect people in any number to have attained to success by age 17, where success is defined as the amassing of a killer resumé, a crushing torrent of accomplishments and distinctions. As you know better than I, expectation creep has remade the world of youth in many parts of our culture, surrounding the really talented, and the fairly talented but really privileged, with hitherto-unimaginable opportunities for the exercise of their gifts, but simultaneously raising the pressure for high performance and spreading it deep into the former domain of play.

None of you is a pure product of this cultural phenomenon, but I doubt that any of you will have been completely immune to it either. You got into college, after all, and in our day college admissions offices are the secret audience for much high achievement in early life. Let me say too that, though I allude to it with a certain skepticism, I recognize that this new feature of the American youth environment has some highly positive aspects. This culture trains people to know the difference between the pretty good and the supremely good in different domains of performance and so supports the taste for excellence. Just as important, living in the presence of expectation helps people make something of themselves. In the face of such demands, people whose life could easily dribble away into the usual puddles of sloth and wasted time learn to embrace the discipline needed to bring skills to a high level, in this way discovering the reach of their powers. Whether it was in scientific research, in writing, in sports, music, or wherever, to the extent that you have developed a taste for excellence and for the discipline needed to attain it, you have come here with the best of preparations.

But the culture of accomplishment can produce other by-products together with these very good ones, and I want to warn you against certain other of its leavings.

One thing that can travel with a high premium on personal achievement is an attitude toward others as people to surpass, people whose function is to admire you with jealousy and amazement as you outdo them yet again. To think that the best use of others is as the audience for your glory would be a huge self-impoverishment, but I do not much worry that you will fall prey to this stupidity. In case you do need to be told, I will tell you that a great luxury of your new life is that you have come to a place where others are interesting and talented too — I'll dare to say it: where other people are in their own ways quite as remarkable as you! One of the lovely things about Yale is that students who are entitled to high self-esteem rejoice instead in each other's accomplishments, both in activities they share and ones that lie far afield. The enjoyment of your fellows will give you great pleasure, but it will also be a powerful means to education. While you are here you will want to open yourself to other members of this community, the more the merrier and the more different from you the better. Entering into their different outlooks will give you a fuller acquaintance with the human field, and working with them will help you learn what people can accomplish together that no one of us could manage on our own.

Along with the trap of self-involvement, the culture of overachieverism also breeds certain kinds of self-limitation and even self-intimidation, and these are a far more serious threat. The enlargement of the desire to do well (or to be seen to do well) produces a corresponding enlargement of the shame felt in not doing well, and this can reinforce the tendency to seek scenes where we seem likely to shine and shun ones where we might fail to shine. This is understandable, but I can think of no more disastrous basis on which to approach your education. In your long and only dimly imaginable future life it will be crucial for you to know many things beyond the subjects you are now fairly certain to be able to ace. If you feel confident that you will never need to understand the action of national economies or of molecular and cellular processes or of global religious systems or of words in a sentence, I assure you, there is very small chance that you will turn out to be right. The short-term gains you win from avoiding things you are allegedly not good at will be offset by the lifelong limitations imposed on you through your refusals of education. In any case, are you absolutely sure you could only ever be interested in or good at the things it was agreed you were good at at age 16, or 14, or 12, or 10? How would you know whether you might now have a knack for acting or computer design or foreign language study or foreign policy debate except by trying? And if, upon trying, you should indeed fail to amaze, would that really be a reason to end it all?

Let me tell you a great secret. The world will care far less about what you did and did not accomplish in your first years of college than your inner demons would like you to believe. By dint of much hard work, you've secured a new life that extends you a million new possibilities for enlightenment and self-enlargement and also a chance to pause a little, in your relentless career of accomplishment, to take stock and take new soundings. Please don't deprive yourself of the enjoyment of the prize you worked so hard to win. Do use this place to consolidate known skills and bring them to higher levels of attainment. But please: use it too as a place for experiment, for exploration, for taking new measures of the world's interests and your powers.

Last and in certain ways most troubling, along with the many benefits the culture of achievement may have brought you, it is possible that it may have induced in you some of the mindlessness it tends to promote toward its own goals. The trouble with habitually scanning the landscape for games one could enter and do well at is that it promotes the thoughtless assumption that these are the games worth playing. But after a while, however proficient you are at some events, you will want to make your own reckoning of what is truly worth your effort, time, and care. I have known Yale students whose schedules were so crowded with commitments as to make the Secretary of State seem like a lady of leisure, and I in part applaud this way of life, since in my experience wisdom is more likely to grow from activity and involvement than from passivity and sloth. But as you construct your new life here, it would be well for you to remember that the goal of your activity is wisdom, not mere busyness, and to take pains to see what your involvements are teaching you. It's quite possible to lead a whole life in successful compliance with some external protocol of success. In Grove Street Cemetery you can see the gravestone of a long-deceased professor listing every degree and prize he won and every university position he held. (The ultimate resumé! I hope it helped him in the next admissions process.) But it would be at least as impressive to have lived up to some thoughtfully achieved personal idea of what makes a valuable life, so I hope you'll take time, here, to think and reflect. If you leave here with a ripened sense of what life seems best worth living, you'll have the accomplishment best worth the accomplishing.

Women and Men of the Class of 2003, I imagine that some of you are now mutinously muttering: "What's this? I've worked so hard to make a success of myself only to have some berobed stranger tell me I've had it all wrong?" But if I've been cruel, as Hamlet said, it was only to be kind. We know and respect your achievements to date, and we are certainly not indifferent to your future attainments. We chose you from 10,000 others because we see in you the capacity to lead important lives, lives of thoughtfulness, creativity, and service in every domain of human effort. But if you are to capture that larger success someday, it will not be because you pursued some relatively timid idea of success while you were in college but because you used this time to open yourself, to expand and explore, to take the fuller measure of your world and of your powers. Follow my prescription, allow yourself to get a real education here, and what you hope for will come to pass. Do this and it will truly be able to be said: he did well at Yale; she did really, really well. Do well. Go well. Welcome to Yale.

WHAT COUNTRY, FRIENDS, IS THIS?

Freshman Address, September 3, 2000

MR. PRESIDENT, colleagues, friends of the shining youth sitting here before me, I welcome you to this great event. Members of the Class of 2004, the 300th class to enter this school, I welcome you to Yale. Judging by the imposing setting and the plumage of the rare birds up on this stage, this is a moment for high pomp and ceremony. I won't deny its solemnity, but I would have thought the right mood for this occasion was festive, and I could hardly blame you, Yale's newest recruits, if you were to let out a whoop of joy. As of this moment, you have a fresh start, a fresh page on which to write the story of your life. Everything you've worked for all those years lies open before you. Everything you're proud of from your previous life comes forward with you as a tested strength, and everything you'd just as soon forget is left far behind, never to be even suspected by your new friends. For us the pleasure is no less. This is a school that rejoices in its students and the energy and creativity they bring. You are our freshpersons, that's to say our *fresh persons*, people full of vigorous, undiminished life. Men and Women of the Class of 2004, enter, enjoy, and invigorate this place.

By chance or fate, when I first began thinking about this gathering three or four weeks ago, an image came to mind that has continued to haunt me, supplying my first vision of you and your arrival. At the beginning of the second scene of Shakespeare's *Twelfth Night*—this scene is also wittily alluded to at the end of the film *Shakespeare in Love*—a young woman comes ashore at a place she's never been and says: "What country, friends, is this?"

I recognize the limits of Viola's entrance as an image for your arrival. There are differences, I admit. Shakespeare's heroine was cast ashore by a shipwreck that only she and a few companions (or so it would seem) survived. In the Yale rewrite of *Twelfth Night*, we would have to imagine Viola being delivered in some oversized motor vehicle, and outfitted not with a stick of driftwood but with box upon box of personal necessities, including uncountable CDs. Viola arrives on the sands of Illyria with no idea where she is and no one to greet her. In the Yale version she would be received with almost ludicrous hospitality. She might already have spent a weekend or two the preceding spring testing out this possible future home in some version of Future Freshman Days. (Called what: Impending Illyria Days?) She might already have tromped around the outskirts of Illyria with pleasant and reassuring companions on any of several preorientation programs or preseason warm-ups. She would certainly have had her ship greeted by teams of grinning upperclassmen who ran out to make sure she didn't have to carry the least splinter of driftwood to her room. She would then be welcomed by freshman counselors, honored at multiple receptions, and treated to days of formal orientation, in case any questions remained.

I speak with humor of Yale's nuclear-powered welcome wagon, but I'm happy that it exists. Among other things, it conveys a message it's important for you to learn: though this is indeed a place for the high-powered and overachieving, it's also a place where people look out for each other and take the trouble to be kind. But behind this barrage of hospitality, and behind your air of already seeming completely at home here, I'll wager that what you are at bottom is what Shakespeare showed in Viola: a young person on the edge of a terra incognita, a person crossing to a strange new land and life. What could be more natural at this moment than to engage in a kind of orgy of reacculturation, struggling to make this place a known, even native, land! But what I want to say to you, as you crawl up the shores of Yale, is not to be so dismissive of the experience of foreignness. You'll find Yale to be quite a homey place, but in some serious sense *dis*orientation, defamiliarization, is the most valuable thing Yale has to offer.

Humans are innately curious, which means that we have a positive craving for expanded knowledge and deepened understanding. But this urge is opposed by countervailing drives that are no less deeply human — not least, our urge to cluster into communities of local consensus, little worlds of shared understanding where questions can't be grasped as questions because some answer has been accepted as self-evident. Education proceeds through the reopening of closed questions, and this requires the breaking of preconceptions and incorporation of alien points of view. Human creativity has always been strongest where groups with different mental horizons have collided, their interaction enabling a breakthrough that neither side could achieve on its own. John Darnell, who teaches Near Eastern Languages and Literatures at Yale, found evidence last year of the oldest-known use of an alphabet, a use almost 400 years earlier than any documented before. But Darnell's discovery also suggests that the written alphabet came into being through the crossing of cultural bounds. His find evokes an image of Egyptian military scribes coming into contact with outlanders who had come into Egypt from elsewhere in the Middle East. In the exchange that followed, it would appear, the scribes drew on a technology their people knew, the written hieroglyphic, but altered it in order to register the alien names of foreigners — who could then learn this easily mastered, rough-and-ready writing system and put it to their own uses.

We could find a comparable history of cross-cultural collaboration in the birth of the great new technology of this time, the World Wide Web. In an abbreviated version of this story, the computer scientist who originated the notion of packet switching — a form of communication that could send chunks of a message through a distributed network rather than passing it in one lump through a dedicated line — sold the American military on this concept. The military developed this idea by building the ARPANET, whose use was extended to certain research universities. (Dot edu, in the address your friends will soon know you by, was originally the companion not of the famous dot com and dot org but of dot mil: this was the educational component of a primarily military system.) This highly specialized creation achieved the potential for a more general life when scientists at CERN, the high-energy particle physics facility in Geneva, Switzerland, developed the hypertext markup language that allowed freer communication across networks. As this invention was further elaborated by people from yet other origins working with other purposes, the ARPANET built to exchange esoteric government-funded research was transformed into the Internet we know—a collaborative creation that no single party had seen the possibility of on its own.

Having myself come to this strange new place some years ago, I know how eager you might be to fit in and catch on. (I am a person who almost missed meals in my first freshman hours because I thought the Freshman Commons was the New Haven train station. Orientation has its privileges!) But having been here awhile, I know that the great gift this place extends to you is ready access to the unfamiliar. The unknown, what lies outside your current ken, is the place for discovery and self-enlargement—that is, for education. What this great educational establishment offers you is a million doors out of the prison of your insularity. But let's not assume that living in the neighborhood of the foreign is an automatic route to education. For every case where the crossing of cultures has produced an alphabet or an Internet, there are a dozen where it has created reciprocal dread, hostility, and a recoil into a tight, narrow version of one's side. In ways less harmful but not much less stupid, many moderns have learned to venture into the space of the foreign and even pretend to take a little interest in it, all the while—like the American tourists who rush to find Kentucky Fried Chicken as soon as they land in Beijing—keeping their insularity studiously intact.

For the unfamiliar to become a source of education, it has to be approached with authentic openness. Openness involves removing mental obstructions to what's outside, like prejudice and preconception. But the openness I'm speaking of is not only a matter of passive accessibility. It requires an active reach outside, a willingness to project yourself out into the unfamiliar, to enter into it sufficiently to see the different way things look from its different position. It then requires you to bring an alien outlook back to bear on your initial understanding — so as to highlight the limits of your assumptions, to supplement them with fuller knowledge, or to win a more conscious, tested sense of why you think the thing you do. You got into Yale, but to get a Yale education you'll need to practice the arts of self-opening: to learn to tolerate and even cultivate the leaving of known worlds.

It occurs to me there are people in this room who will warmly agree with everything I've said but then go out and defy my teachings, without being aware that they are doing so. So to make my message harder to mistake, I will stoop to a few particulars. You've taken the trouble to get into a school that offers nearly two thousand undergraduate courses, and where virtually everything can be studied in extraordinary depth. Now, I suppose, some of you will want to figure out how much of this rich offering you can succeed in avoiding. My colleagues and I have known students to hope to excuse themselves from entire domains of knowledge with profundities like "I'm not a science person" or "I read a poem once and didn't like it" or "I'm not good at languages" or "I'm just not good with numbers." (To which I reply: You should have told us this before!) Avoiding everything that doesn't comes easy would be a good way to pick your courses if the point of college were to be pleasant, but if you want an education, you'll need a different approach. You'll need to seek out the things you haven't already mastered, to look for new chances and challenges, even to take some risks — and I certainly hope you will.

At Yale your classmates can give an education quite as powerful as formal coursework. But again, that depends on how you approach them — how willing you are to venture into newfound lands. We've all looked at distant parts of the world where people can't figure out how to get along and have felt sadness but also secret smugness, knowing that we would never be guilty of such stupidity. Now it's for you to actually see if you can live together in a better way. You've just come together in a community of strangers. Your rooms, I know, are delightfully spacious, but for all that, you're packed together with a certain density. To make the best of your new state, you're going to need to practice tolerance for people you might initially find strange or annoying, and to figure out how to be less annoying to those you yourself might annoy.

But tolerance and courtesy are limited virtues and should be seen as minimal goals. To get an education out of those who surround you, you're going to need to go out to them and enter into their point of view, the more the merrier and the more different from yours the better — also, to make yourself available as an education for them. Like the travelers I mocked before, you could manage to remain quite insular at Yale if you confined your friendships to human flavors you already know and like. But if you'd come to a place where you could share the company of bright, energetic people from every origin, of every belief, with every known interest, who are right there around you for you to enjoy, how could you want to miss that chance? Unless you were very foolish, you couldn't — but you have to actively extend yourself to seize this opportunity.

Last let me note that there is another provincialism quite as impoverishing as any social or academic one. In our world there are all kinds of people willing to pay tribute to diversity who have no intention of letting difference ever change their minds. "Conviction" is a name for our most deeply held values and beliefs, but conviction can bring limits along with its values, since conviction can breed the certainty that you are right and those so misguided as to disagree with you are wrong — so wrong that you would scarcely even want to know such people, let alone engage them or listen to them. I trust that you have convictions and I applaud you for them, but I hope you don't come here with the assumption that you already know the final answer to any question and have nothing to learn from the non-like-minded. Learned Hand said of the First Amendment that "it presupposes that right conclusions are more likely to be gathered out of a multitude of tongues, than through any authoritative selection," and this university emphatically shares this belief. In this conception, truth requires searching, an act of open, unforeclosed inquiry, that is best conducted in the midst of plural and competing possibilities, since (as Hand said) "it is only by cross-lights from varying directions that full illumination can be secured." For the sake of your growing wisdom, instead of insulating yourselves with those who already exactly agree with you, you will need not just to tolerate but to seek the company of those who differ with you, and find out what they actually think. Argument and exchange are the stuff of education; well-guarded unanimity is not.

What country, friends, is this? When Viola came ashore and asked that question, a grizzled veteran, a sea captain, was there to fill her in a little. But you know what? She scarcely needed his advice, as you scarcely need mine. The place she landed was an unknown land, but she was plucky and resourceful, and by the end of a short scene she had taken the measure of this new site and set out to get the good of it. I choose her as your emblem because I think no less of you. Bright, energetic, enterprising, ingenious, who if not you could do this place right? Friends, this is a good country, with much to offer and no requirement but that you exploit it to the fullest. Come determined to explore new territory with a certain adventurousness and your story will have a happy ending. When we meet here again at the end of fifth act of your Yale career, you'll have enriched your grasp of yourself and your world and will be ready to take up an active, constructive part in the life of your times. Confident that you want the very thing I've required of you, I can deliver my exit line. Men and Women of the Yale College Class of 2004, you are welcome to these shores.

OF PREPARATION
FOR AN UNKNOWN WORLD

Freshman Address, September 1, 2001

I HAVE A SPECIAL message for each seating zone. To those behind me in the choice seats on stage: Mr. President, colorful colleagues, another year begins. Welcome back to our inspiring work. Turning now to the first balcony and the yet more exalted nosebleed section of this great hall: Parents of our new class, I rejoice with you on this happy day. With your help and support, your young friend has got into one of the great universities in this land. More significant by far, with your loving assistance, this child has grown into the sort of a person who deserves the challenges of this place, a person of shining character and promise. So far so good! You've done your work well. I welcome you to the family of Yale.

Last I turn to this mass of youth who would already look just like Yale students if you weren't so curiously well dressed. What can I say to you? Only that I rejoice in your arrival and exult as you start your new life. If I remember right, you had an ordeal ahead at this time last year. You had grades to make, tests to take, the whole anxious task of trying to seem like the outstanding person you hoped we would take you for. Good news: it worked! And now you're here, with nothing to do but to enjoy your prize. An almost inconceivable luxury is about to surround you: spacious accommodations no doubt already being turned into designer showcases; almost infinitely rich academic and extra-academic opportunities; and the greatest of luxuries, a selection of the most talented and high-spirited of your contemporaries to stimulate you and be your friends. We will celebrate Yale's 300th birthday this October, but though many cohorts have preceded you, as of this day, Yale is yours. Yale College Class of 2005, enjoy the riches of this place.

That was the easy part of this address; now I face a problem. I'm painfully aware that when officials speak on ceremonious occasions, what in their own minds reads like the generous gift of wisdom can seem to the audience like a blast of sententious wind. Being a literature professor, I know the great prototype of the well-meaning elder giving advice to the college-bound: it's Polonius, the tedious windbag in Shakespeare's *Hamlet*. But though I would never have chosen that role model, I do want to say something serious about your new venture – so be prepared.

In the modern world, virtually every country has devised a means for sorting out youth of outstanding promise and sending them on for further training. In the great majority of places, this is a moment of specialization. It's assumed that you have already found the field that will provide the best outlet for your particular powers, and you go to college to master that domain. In a leading university in Beijing, where I was two weeks ago, I learned that students not only apply to a major and are admitted to the study of a major when they apply to college but that they then live together with their fellow concentrators, averting distraction from the chosen point.

Yale embraces a different philosophy. Yale's version of education combines some measure of specialization with a countervailing breadth, multiple cross-trainings of the developing mind. The ideal of many-sided education appears in our distributional requirements but in a hundred other ways as well. Witness Yale's frantic extracurricular scene, which supplements formal academics with many other kinds of training. Witness our housing arrangements, designed to ensure that you live together with and learn from people who have nothing in common except their energy and talent. Further, though some of you have already found your life mission, we neither require nor expect that our students will already know the line their life will trace. Education is here conceived as a space of discovery. If a student changes her mind about what matters to her and strikes out in new direction, we regard it a sign that education is taking place.

To eyes trained in a scheme like ours, the system that favors single focus and fixed direction will seem imprisoning, rigidifying, the training ground of the narrow mind. But our system may seem comparably bizarre from a different point of view. Some foreigners see our plan of education as pointlessly indulgent, protracting the freedoms of adolescence when you should be in serious training for worldly careers. Liberal education can come in for criticism from our own culture as well. Two years ago, in the hottest days of the self-proclaimed New Economy, I was assured that no really intelligent college-age person would be found wasting his days in such pursuits when he could be out founding his own corporate empire. In times of economic downturn we're told that liberal education is all very nice but what students really need are marketable skills.

If we continue the practice of liberal education, it is not because we think its merits are beyond discussion. It is because, whatever challenges it is subjected to, this plan continues to show its power to meet deep personal and social needs.

Yale's version of education has two justifications. First, it's our belief that in future it will be important for you not just to get a decent job but also to lead a decent life, and we think that college should help toward both goals, not the first alone. It is a sad fact but true that people your age learn things relatively easily that can later be mastered only with great pain, and that the gifts we develop in our youth become permanent powers of the mature self. Psychologists tell us that the human self begins to consolidate itself (I assume this is a euphemism for harden) in the early and mid-20s, and that the more the potentialities of personality that have been activated by that point, the richer the selfhood that can be pulled together. If this is true, then it matters how vigorously and variously you exercise your powers, and it also matters what a school asks of you. When we encourage you to broaden your knowledge, act out your talents, and expand the range of your human acquaintance and social sympathies, it's so that you can bring a more flexible, more capable self into the world.

Though we are not narrowly fixed on it, we aren't uninterested in the question of your future careers. But here too it is our belief that a broad, exploratory education gives a superior preparation to one with a tight vocational aim. The crucial point here is that the world is characterized more and more by dynamism, instability, and chronic and rapid transformations. If you wish to prepare for a life in such a world, then you should be getting ready to act in a world you can't foresee, amid opportunities and challenges that can't be even guessed when the preparation is made. For an experiment, think back with me. I was born in 1947. What would a person starting out in 1947 have known of the coming world? At that point there was still uncertainty about whether the Great Depression would resume now that the Second World War was over. Who foresaw that the history of the next 20 years would instead be one of an unexampled growth and unprecedentedly widespread prosperity? And if they had known that much, who would have known that this rising tide would be accompanied by powerful assaults on systems of official discrimination? A segregationist presidential candidate carried several states in the election of 1948. Who would then have predicted the *Brown v. Board of Education* decision handed down in 1954, or the Montgomery bus boycott of 1955, or the '60s Civil Rights movement—the great historical event of my youth—that delegitimated discrimination first on racial grounds, then also on grounds of gender? These things changed American life so profoundly that a person with a 1947 education would have been at complete loss in the world of my graduation year—the year Yale College announced that it would open its doors to women.

A significant number of you were born in 1983. What would a person at that time have seen ahead? American foreign policy was still largely fixed on Cold War enemies and the proxy wars the Cold War spawned. In 1983 who saw the end of Communist control of Eastern Europe, the collapse of the Soviet

Union, and the birth of a new world order organized around not great power oppositions but transnational economic inter-dependences? In 1983 the computer literate at Yale did their work on the Yale mainframe. Who foresaw the personal computer, the then-uninvented Internet, and all the changes they have brought to global and personal life?

My point is simple. You're going to have a career after Yale. It's not for us to say what you'll do then. Our only wish is that you give a thoughtful, constructive life to your times in any of the thousand forms in which such lives are needed. If we were to train you in the skills of some existing career, we would not only have severely delimited your future competence. In a world so full of changes, we might well have made you an anachronism, a well-trained practitioner of some vanished art. Our gamble is that we can best prepare you by developing deep skills that are specific to no work but of use in any work, which you can deploy in a versatile way on the changing facts of your world. What might these include? Such breadth of knowledge that whatever fact or problem you encounter, you'll be able to set it within a broader understanding; the ability to pay the kind of attention and apply the kind of analytical pressure that bring discoveries to light; the capacity to express your thoughts clearly and advance them with force; being imaginative and taking the initiative, and so creating a possibility where none was evident before; not least, being aware of yourself as a member of a community and using your powers for the common good.

If this sounds platitudinous, let me give an example of what I mean. The first person from China to graduate from an American university was a Yalie: Yung Wing, of the Yale College Class of 1854. When he came here, Yung Wing had an offer to pay his full fare if he would agree to return to China as a missionary. He declined, on the grounds that he did not want his life's work delimited for him in advance. After he graduated, he returned to China, where he worked rather aimlessly as a translator, then as a clerk in a tea house, when — in recognition of his verbal powers — he was asked to write an appeal for foreign aid after a major flood. This plus his entrepreneurial ventures getting tea out of the rebel-held areas won him notice as a clever man. In consequence, Yung Wing was asked to advise the Chinese government on how to close the knowledge gap in the field of technology. He at this point returned to the United States (stopping at his tenth Yale reunion en route) to buy machine tools for China, equipment that, on Yung Wing's advice, could manufacture not just specific needs but the machinery to meet many further needs—steamboats, for instance, in addition to rifles. Having established a base for technological education in China, he pioneered educational exchanges between the United States and China, and was then asked—in an early human rights initiative—to document abuses of Chinese migrant laborers in the New World, in a report that ended the slave-like trade in coolie labor with Peru. Later still, he drew up plans for a national bank.

Now I ask: How was he able to participate so constructively in so many different domains? Not by having been trained in a specialized way for any of them. He could move from one newly arising situation to another and play a creative role in each because he was smart and plucky and had a highly various, highly mobile set of skills—just like you, when we get done with you!

You now know what we have in mind for you. But the main thing I need to tell you is, it takes you to make it happen. So let me beg you to use this place in the way that will give you the good of it. Polonius-like at last, let me offer some bits of advice, First, don't be passive. An anonymous sage has written that "Life is not a spectator sport," and still less is Yale. This place gives its rewards to those who take the initiative, those who seek out contacts and opportunities. Being a little forward won't be held against you here; being a little bashful is a way to rob yourself of interesting chances. Second, I hope you'll be venturesome in this new life. To build the broadly capable future you, you need to open yourself up, to try new things, even things—horrors!—at which you may not excel. If you stick to the safety of the things you're already good at, you'll develop powers, but not the range of powers that might be yours. I commend to you this motto from *Moby-Dick*: "I try all things; I achieve what I can."

In the same vein, you need the courage to take on things that may be hard for you. Every one of you who plays a sport or a musical instrument knows that discipline is the means to increased power, the price we pay to build a knack into a high-performing capacity. Since you've already learned so much the hard way, might I hope that you'll be a little scornful of the easy way – and not, for instance, shun whole domains of knowledge because they feel like work? (For shame!)

Finally, I urge you to have some ambitions of your own for your education and not to forfeit the task to us. You will not have lived up to our expectations if you merely meet our requirements. What we want of you is that you make some interesting personal use of this place: that you use Yale to build a distinctive self and life.

You have heard, I'm sure, of an enterprise zone – a place where governments give tax breaks to encourage business to settle. In brooding on your coming, I thought to take this phrase in its radical sense. In its full meaning, an enterprise is a bold or momentous undertaking, and an enterprising person is someone energetic, high-spirited, and willing to run risks for the sake of high rewards. You stand on the brink of a new life; it's yours to decide what to make of it. If you take my words seriously, you will make Yale College your personal enterprise zone: a place of energetic activity and spirited attempt. Men and Women of the Class of 2005, I welcome you to this undertaking, which will pay off in proportion as you approach it boldly. This place is yours now. Come get the good of it.

LEARNING BY CHOICE
AND BY CHANCE

Freshman Address, August 31, 2002

SHORTLY AFTER I began thinking about this occasion, the *New York Times* carried a story about the spacecrafts Voyager 1 and 2. Launched more than 20 years ago, these crafts have taught us most of what we know of Jupiter, Saturn, and Neptune and, having passed far beyond Pluto, they are poised to make the first human register of the heliopause, the outer edge of the solar system. This story put me in mind of those rocket launches that once made great theater with their rhythm of countdown, liftoff, then that curious moment when the booster rocket broke off as the spacecraft continued to ascend. And that made me think of you.

Parents and families, this is a time of pride, happiness, and grief. We greet you but we also say farewell to you, since when this ceremony is over, it's time for you to go. Why? In the logic of my metaphor, it's time to uncouple and drop away because you have done your work. The energies of your love and care helped put this precious payload in orbit. Your success is proved by the fact that it will now carry on on its own.

And Yale's new arrivals, our 302nd class, what does my bizarrely protracted metaphor say for you? As of this moment, you are flying free; from here forward, your business is just to soar. Up to this point a great deal of your education has been introductory or foundational, and hemmed in with restriction. Now you reach the good part, when you can do the interesting things you spent all those years preparing for. To your families I say hail and farewell, but to you I say hail and hooray. Men and Women of the Class of 2006, welcome to Yale, and to a great phase of your life.

Now a few words about what's up ahead.

What do we know about you? We know for sure that you were good at getting into college. At your young age, you have mastered some very advanced skills, like the art of presenting yourselves with appealing modesty while making sure that we learn of every one of your killer accomplishments. What do we hope of you? In choosing you from thousands of others, our bet was that you will be men and women who will contribute in special measure to the good of your times. Your early accomplishments were important to us less in themselves than as signs of the intelligence, energy, creativity, and concern for others you might someday put at the service of your world, in any of the thousand forms in which such powers are needed.

Now how are you going to get from the promise you have already shown to its fulfillment in later life? Your college years could help make this difference. Let's ask exactly how.

While reflecting on this question, I happened on a magazine piece on the designer of the Vietnam Veterans Memorial in Washington, D.C. (You must be thinking that my intellectual life is almost wholly at the mercy of the contents of my mailbox.) The Vietnam Memorial is one of the most powerful works of civic commemoration to have been created in modern times, and it is all the more remarkable because it was produced under a double difficulty. Since it was designed to be built near other famous monuments like the Lincoln Memorial, one challenge was how to interpolate a new, contemporary structure into this tradition-heavy space without creating a jarring dissonance or an empty repetition of classical cliches. The harder challenge was how to commemorate something that was the object of such intense, unresolved ambivalence: how to build a monument that would speak to those who had believed in the war and those who had thought it a huge, violent mistake, those who had risked their lives in the nation's service only to find themselves reviled for their sacrifice and those who had risked exile or criminal conviction for their opposition to this cause.

The problem was solved by a design whose aesthetic presence carries the viewer far beyond the partisan register: a work of grave visual austerity that registers the name of each American who died in the war on a low, black granite wall, refusing any statement but the one everyone could assent to: that, right or wrong, the war had exacted a steep human cost; and that each individual death was a proper object for grief, memory, and respect.

The design for the Vietnam Memorial was selected through an open competition, and as you may know but the judges certainly did not, the submitter of the winning proposal was a Yale student, an undergraduate who created her design in a seminar and made an early model out of mashed potatoes in a Yale dining hall. This was Maya Lin, Yale College Class of 1981, whose work you may also know from the Civil Rights Memorial in Montgomery, Alabama, or the Women's Table one block from here. Let's use Maya Lin as an example of someone who sat in this room as an arriving freshman and later used her gifts to meet an important social need. What road led from here to there?

It's natural to assume that this person always knew that she was on her way to becoming the famous architect Maya Lin and knew just the path that would lead to this inevitable success. But if you read the profile in the July 8 *New Yorker*, you will learn something quite different. We learn that she came to Yale with the thought of becoming (are you ready?) a field zoologist. She backed away when she learned that dissection would be involved, and — now I quote — "She didn't know, at first, what to do instead; but she loved art and she loved math — so, she explained, architecture seemed perfect."* This new revelation must not have come to her too promptly, however, since we also learn that she took no architecture courses until her third year at Yale — suggesting considerable groping before she found the light.

---

* Louis Menand, "The Reluctant Memorialist," *The New Yorker*, July 8, 2002, pp. 55–65. The quote is from page 58.

I find this a brilliant if extreme example of an important truth. When this school is used right, students don't just fill in a schedule with more or less interchangeable courses. They bring their interests to bear on their courses, they use their classes to bring their interests to a higher development. But this process does not always lead to the expected result. Lin found her eventual course by plotting an initial course but then engaging in self-revising, open-ended exploration. Through her pursuit of known interests she discovered new interests, and with them new knowledge of what she could do and be.

Even then, Lin's relevant education did not proceed from one source or decision. The profile highlights many aspects of her college experience that seem to feed directly into her later accomplishments but that could have formed part of no plan when they occurred. It would not be easy to have guessed that this child of Chinese émigrés would have taken a junior term abroad in Denmark. While there, Lin studied in the section of Copenhagen that contains the large cemetery where notables like Kierkegaard and Hans Christian Andersen are buried, which Danes use as a public park. Taking in this fact gave further definition to Lin's emerging focus — it sharpened her interest in memorial spaces and their role in everyday life — but Lin did not go to Denmark to make this discovery. On her way to one goal, she took in something peripheral, which she wove together with other perceptions in an amassing harmony of recognitions. The very space you walked through to get to this assembly figured in her retrospectively purposeful, initially fortuitous education. The Woolsey Hall rotunda, Yale's great pedestrian shortcut, is another place of daily use carved with names of those dead in wars. Thousands pass through this space unseeingly every day. But Lin saw it, brought her interests to bear into it, and carried it up into her active understanding, where, joined with other deposits in wholly unforeseen ways, it would one day help her imagine a monument of her own.

As you've surely guessed, this talk is not about Maya Lin at all. It's about education, where it comes from and how it happens; and though I speak of her education, it's yours that I have in mind. Your education will share none of the specific content of Lin's, but it could share its form. As you come to full maturity, this place gives you the chance to forge a richer sense of the world and a deeper grasp of the powers you could bring to bear. How will this happen to the fullest extent? Lin's case suggests three replies. You'll get the good of this place to the extent that you engage it actively and intentionally; to the extent that you explore the field of possibilities flexibly and broadly; and to the extent that you open yourself to new experience in the widest possible array.

To be a little more particular, you could succeed in getting very little from this place if you approach it with passivity, an eagerness to follow the many, or the willingness just to do what we ask. Maya Lin met all of Yale's formal requirements, but meeting those requirements never made anyone a Maya Lin. She realized the possibilities of this place by bringing an active, distinctive curiosity to bear on them, and she sought out opportunities that were not lying in plain sight. It was Lin and her classmates, not the instructor, who initiated the seminar in which she first designed the memorial.

Docility and inertia aren't common Yale diseases, so I don't much worry about you on that score. But I am more concerned by another threat, the dangers of an understandable timidity. If you're like every other group of freshmen who ever came here, behind the mask of your fabulous self-possession are likely to be deep reserves of anxiety, and these may drive you toward the typical recourse of the vulnerable and exposed: the urge to construct a tight, safe, controllable version of Yale to ward off the terrors of your new home. I have heard of students who, from the whole ludicrous cornucopia of our academic offerings, have sought to take those courses most like ones they have taken before, to fend off the terrors of the new. I've known students who, from the whole company of gifted humanity we've assembled around you, have tried to restrict their social exposure to the very types they already know — people from their same country, same kind of school, same religion, same cultural background, same team sport, and on and on.

If you feel such temptations, I have good news and bad news. The good news is, Yale is a benign environment, very friendly, very supportive. Though some things will seem strange at first, it's safe to come out: no one is waiting to pounce on your real or imagined deficiencies. The bad news is, in this new home, hiding out in supposedly safe places is impoverishing in the extreme. Besides the tedium of all that familiarity, every new experience you shut yourself off from — every intellectual challenge you succeed in not facing, every unfamiliar social type you succeed in not knowing — is a chance for discovery you have succeeded in shutting down. Some set of these experiences could be your version of Maya Lin's junior year in Denmark or walk through Woolsey Hall: the thing that fatefully enlarged you and gave you more fully to yourself. But that's not going to happen unless you open yourself to new things and the lessons they could teach.

Finally, if you want a real education, you can't be excessively concerned to chart it all in advance. It is an illusion that successful people move toward their goals along straight lines. As the Maya Lin case shows, the process through which people realize their promise is fed by a hundred sources foreseen and unforeseen, working together in unguessable ways, toward ends that are partly planned, partly surprising. You have been very successful at a young age and much of your success has probably clustered around some statement about who you are: I'm a great (fill in the blank: cellist; high jumper; filmmaker; teacher of underprivileged children); I'm going to be a great (fill in the blank: biomedical researcher; environmental lawyer; poet; software entrepreneur). These are excellent ambitions and you should not hasten to give them up. But the use of this place is to build a broader knowledge and enable a more knowing choice, even if you choose the same goal you already have in mind; so while I would not have you give in to whims, you need be willing to wander outside your appointed line — even if it leads away from the paths of your confident success. If Maya Lin had hewed to the line she traced in advance, she would not have found the passion we think of as her identity and might now be the manager of a petting zoo. If she had let external measures dictate what she was good at, she might have been misled another way: amazingly, the design that won the national competition received only a B+ when she submitted in her course. She found her thing by trying many things and by having the courage of her curiosity—and so, I trust, will you.

Women and Men of the Yale College Class of 2006, you worked hard to get into a great college. And you succeeded! And this day you get your reward. But though your work to date will serve you well, the reward is not the chance to repeat your success on identical terms. It is the chance to reopen your mind, to renegotiate your interests, to win a deeper purchase on yourself and your world—and to make this happen, you need to embrace both the disciplines and the freedoms of this place. Seek out all the opportunities of your new home and you won't be the same person when you leave. You'll be you, all right, but you enriched and developed: you further realized through the process of education. The riches of this place are now all yours. Let the education begin!

WORDS AT MIDTERM

Freshman Address, October 11, 2003

Note: In the fall of 2003, the original Freshman Assembly
was canceled because of a labor action and rescheduled for
Parents' Weekend.

IN A CUSTOM observed since time immemorial, the Freshman
Assembly is held on the first full day after students arrive at
Yale. With its pomp and solemnity, this event serves at least
three important ceremonial functions. First, it thanks parents
for raising the prodigies who will now be our students and
readies them for the hard work of saying goodbye. Second, it
marks the official moment of entry of new students into Yale
College, as a symmetrical ceremony four years later will mark
their exit. Third and most crucially, this ceremony does the
work of orientation, conjuring an inspiring vision to guide students in their education and give their life here point.

Funny thing: none of this happened this year! For reasons
you may remember, this year's addresses have to take their
model from the belated birthday card, the genre of greetings
that are very sincere but a little late. So with the blush of the
delinquent, let me say to the families here assembled, six weeks
after it would have been the right time to say it: Welcome to
Yale! and to our students, long after you've begun to make
yourselves at home, Make yourself right at home!

What does it mean for this ceremony to take place not upon
arrival but half a term after the fact? For the families who are
able to be present today, the difference is a good one. By a mira-

73

cle of rescheduling, we've changed what would have been a day of doleful partings into a mass family reunion, the fifth act in some ultimate Shakespearean comedy. I trust that you have found the kid you left here six weeks ago to be basically the same yet mysteriously enhanced: already a little smarter and more mature.

For you, though, my friends in the Class of 2007, the meaning of this rescheduling is far more troubling. For six weeks I have wondered in agony what has it meant for you to be deprived of the guidance the President and I were so superbly equipped to provide. Robbed of your Freshman Assembly, I can only assume you have been like kids given the car without benefit of driver's education: wreaking havoc on yourselves and others, doomed to run amok. In truth, you seem to be doing fine — seldom has a class caught onto this place with greater ease and less fuss; but this fact is to me more troubling still. Could it be that you were able to figure this place out perfectly well without wisdom from the likes of me? The notion would be shocking if it were not so obviously implausible.

Since we're together at last, I will not spare you a few words — though since I've never addressed a class at this point in its career, you'll have to bear with me as I try to guess what's right to say. I have some sense of what the right message is on the day of arrival. When, after all that preparation and anxious waiting, students finally arrive at college, it's a time of almost miraculous expansion. So many new opportunities solicit your interest and engagement, so many new freedoms are suddenly yours. It's both completely exhilarating and completely daunting, so at that point my message to you would have been: take advantage of this place; plunge in; don't hang back; seize all the chances that now surround you.

But if you obeyed the orders I was not here to give, and you probably have, by now you've likely reached a second phase. You've got to know scores of people the likes of whom you've never met before; you've opened yourself to Yale's slightly overwhelming curricular riches; you've taken up tutoring or giving music lessons in local schools, and joined some team with a bizarrely demanding practice schedule, and tried out for a play or founded a comedy group or juggling troupe, in addition to all those further chances for education that high administrators barely suspect. (I have recently learned of the formidable expertise developing in Bingham Hall in Dance Dance Revolution, not yet an accredited academic program.) This life is all extremely exhilarating. But it's cumulatively pretty exhausting, and you will not be the first person I've met who might be feeling, about now, that this new life is growing seriously untenable – that it's all too much, there's just too much to do, that your choices have put demands on you that aren't compatible with one another or with any sort of a healthy life.

If you have reached such a pass, I have a message for you: It's going to be all right. You were not wrong to open yourself to the opportunities of this place: that's where education comes from. Now you're going to have to learn to cope with the consequences of all that opportunity, but that's an education too: an education in life-definition and in the arts of choice. Hard though it may be to believe at certain hours, you'll make a manageable version of your life at Yale, like thousands before you who felt the same way. But the moment of consolidation has its own dangers, so as you enter it, I'd offer this word of advice. By all means create a workable life at Yale; but don't make that life too insular or reductive. What you're establishing now should be your base camp – something to support ongoing exploration, not the limit of your travel or the end of your road.

To be a little more particular: You have now successfully passed through the ordeal of Yale course selection. Faced with all those choices, you've put together (I trust) a schedule that's prudently composed and conformable to all known rules of schedule formation. So far so good! But I worry that the moves you made to master that challenge might harden into thoughtless habits, unconsciously robbing you of opportunities for your mind. When people come to this campus, they think they'll be lost in its physical vastness and complexity, but that never happens. They work out their personal routine, which dictates a personal itinerary, which means that they always go to certain places and never go to others—which is excellent for the purposes of convenience, but not so great if you wanted to know what all lies around you. You are on the verge of forming your own academic routines, and as you do so, I urge you to recognize and resist the restrictions they embody. There's too much that's interesting to know out there for you to be content always taking certain subjects and never taking others. To get an education, you have to make a point of trying the things you have not yet mastered and exploring the things you don't yet understand. You'll get more good from your program of study if, in choosing your courses, you'll ask not just whether they meet at a comfortable hour and at a convenient distance but how they help build an educated mind.

On another note, the admissions office has searched the four corners of the earth to find interesting contemporaries to be your companions. I'm sure you have not been immune to the excitement of their energy and talent. But all that novelty is exhausting too, and after awhile it's natural to begin to consolidate your personal world—to run your own admissions process for inclusion in your inner circle. I don't doubt that you'll have great friends at this place, and no one who ever went to Yale will fail to understand that at a school like this, friendship is an essential medium of education. But before you hang out your No Vacancy sign, take care not to build your social world in too restrictive a fashion.

It's very easy to allow some one dimension of our existence—the background we come from, the subject we study, the party we favor, the sport we play—to shape our associations without realizing how much it is negating or excluding other possible associations. But the limits of social openness have both a social and a personal cost. History will remember the year you went to college as the year when the United States Supreme Court upheld the legality of affirmative action in college admissions. This policy was upheld on the grounds that it serves to create a convincing openness in the paths to social leadership as well as an enrichment in the experience of education itself. In a powerful dissent well worth your reading, affirmative action is derided as a "classroom aesthetics," a kind of interior decorating scheme masking as a philosophy of education. And it is truer than many like to admit that if the urge to create an inclusive student body were only a matter of adjusting visual appearances, the logic of the court's majority would be seriously eroded. A various student body – and I have in mind a student body various not just along lines of race or ethnicity but along every conceivable human dimension – is of educational value just to the extent that people actually teach each other through the play of difference, and that requires real, deep, and continual interaction. The final guarantor of such interaction will never be the government or the courts. It is the openness toward others of actual individuals: men and women, you and me, making their choices day by day.

When I ask you to resist homogenizing your world, I have one thing in mind more than any other. Above all, don't limit your associations to people who agree with you. While thinking about this talk I was reflecting on the very different picture we saw when students came to school here three short years ago. In the palmy days of the New Economy, child investors were reported to make killings in the stock market during passing periods in high school, and an enchanted nation faced such agonizing issues as what to do with a massive federal surplus, what would happen when unemployment reached zero, and how quickly other nations would follow down the inevitable path to free-market prosperity and Western-style democracy. Well, problems that were temporarily veiled then are back in plain sight now, and today's world poses very different questions. Economically, we live in a time of slow growth but not job growth. How can the engines of prosperity be reignited, and how can the global economy yield the most good for the greatest number with the least attendant social and environmental cost? It's our fate to wake up to almost daily news of bombings throughout the world. How can humans secure themselves against violence, and can they adequately secure themselves without fueling the very hatred they had hoped to quell?

These are damnably difficult questions, but another piece

of recent news could make them even harder than they need to be. I read that American political parties are concluding that the old electoral strategy of first playing to the core adherents and true believers, then reaching out to the independent or unpersuaded, might now be passé, and that parties will succeed best by continuing to appeal to the party base. This may be good politics, but I doubt it's good for the quality of thought that will result from politics. Who do we suppose will be able to deal more constructively with the challenges of our time: people who have only ever experienced preaching to the converted, or people who tested their understanding against the countervailing understandings of others?

Though very new here, you have already been on campus for two periods of controversy. When you came for Bulldog Days last April, there was uproar from clashing responses to the Iraq War. This fall you arrived in the middle of a labor dispute. I might have preferred to show Yale in a calm, pastoral light, and I do regret any inconvenience that you suffered. (As for what you really did with those rebate checks, our inspectors are going through your rooms as I speak.) But you know what? Controversy is not an inappropriate activity on a campus; it is, or at least it can be, the very element of education. Controversy isn't educational when immutable positions batter one another with inflexible aggression. But I question whether things are more educational where there is no argument because people have shut themselves in with the like-minded and shut out the other side, and no one dissents because no one remembers there are questions to be asked.

Your growth could be furthered through controversy of the right sort. It will go to your strength and to the growing wisdom of all if you'll engage with difficult issues and say what you understand of them – say it in a way that will not just win the applause of those you already agree with but possibly persuade those who don't yet see what you see. But for controversy to be instructive, you'll need to acknowledge the point where your understanding leaves off and open yourself to others' different, even opposite points of view – and open yourself in the sincere belief that they may have something to teach. Since I became dean I've only heard one line from a student's lips that I found immitigably depressing: "I care so deeply about this issue that I wouldn't even want to know a person who didn't agree with me." Human, all too human, but profoundly antieducational: since education comes not from hunkering down in well-defended camps of agreement but from facing the challenge of other points of view and being open to hear, in them, that part of the truth one's own point of view has not yet managed to contain.

Men and Women of the Yale College Class of '07, Yale's first excitement may be wearing off, but the best part of your time here lies all before you, not behind. Yale is an educational institution, but it's for you to help make this an educational community: a community whose members test and expand each other's powers of understanding through every interaction all day long. Does that sound like a lot to ask? Sure. But would you be content with less? And who if not you is fit to carry out the task? So finish your tests and papers (you will) and get a little rest, because there's bigger work to be done. Women and Men of the Class of 2007, we rejoice to have you as partners in the work of education. I wish you health, happiness, and magnificent self-enlargement in your years at Yale.

ASPECTS
OF EDUCATION

ON ADMINISTRATION

This essay was written the summer after I had been named Dean
but before I began serious work in the position. It represents,
in retrospect, my guess of what the meaning of that work would be.
First printed in *The New Journal*, September 3, 1993.

In early May I was asked if I would write some thoughts for
publication in *The New Journal*. For several reasons I was
pleased to agree. The editor who asked was a former student; I
have a long-standing admiration for this journal, which was
founded by friends of mine in undergraduate years; and the
terms of the request were exceptionally easy – my piece could be
on any subject, and I'd have the whole summer to write it.

The whole summer having flown by, packed with days
when I could have written my piece if only it had seemed a little
more urgent, I now find myself face to face with my task and
learn that it is an abyss of vagueness. I've seldom found it hard
to write on something; but on "Anything"? That's a taller order,
and it takes me back to the misery-inducing "free theme" of my
youth, that open-ended invitation to expose the barrenness of
one's imagination.

The default topic in those long gone days was "how I spent
my summer," which might avail me here. For how I spent my
summer was learning a new territory and giving some reflection
to the kind of job I've undertaken. So a topic presents itself after
all: Preliminary Reflections of Administration Man.

One thing that has come clear to me is how many years one
can spend in a university without paying any attention to its
administration. When I was an undergraduate the Dean of Yale

College was Georges May. Though my classmates and I could easily pick up on the fact that Dean May was the most urbane person one had ever met, his eyes atwinkle with an extraordinary knowingness mysteriously compatible with endless amusement, I did not know three things about what the Dean of Yale College was or did. There had to be one, it seemed, and there my curiosity ended.

When I was in graduate school, during the student revolution of 1970, I, of course, learned the general mistrust of administrations *de rigeur* in that extraordinary season, and protested such callous displays of administrative power as the tree removals necessary to build the Cross Campus Library. But I still had no idea what administration meant in any concrete sense, and my ignorance persisted long after I joined the faculty.

I speak now from a position of somewhat greater knowledge. From this position I judge that my earlier ignorance represented not a real deficiency but a sign that things were working fairly well. For I now suppose that the deep aim of university administration is in some serious sense to make itself disappear: that its real goal is to make it possible for most people most of the time to think about other things.

My late colleague Michael Cooke said to me shortly after he took up the Mastership of Trumbull College: "You know, Dick, all teaching properly culminates in administration." Michael Cooke was given to oracular utterances, and I remember at the time feeling that this statement was no less profound for being wholly enigmatic. Much later in my own career, I know both what he meant and why I would disagree with him. He meant, I suppose, that the same moral passions that make teaching such a satisfying career for some people are what drive such people into the institutional labors that support education. That, I think, is undeniable: I can't imagine the psyche so malformed that it could desire administrative position as an end rather than as a means to serve other ends. But surely the educative will doesn't lead toward administrative culminations in any inevitable or necessary way; quite the reverse.

Yale has a distinguished tradition of scholar-teachers who have come to administrative power on the basis of their work as educators, not bureaucrats. My other colleague lost too soon, A. Bartlett Giamatti, is the great modern exemplum of this type. Yale remains highly distinctive for its refusal to tolerate the separation of administrative from academic personnel. What was once said of men and dust can largely be said of Yale administrators: of the faculty they are, and to the faculty they shall return. Nevertheless, the faculty-administrator tradition can conceal the fact that the great majority of faculty do not, do not want to, do not need to, turn away from educational to administrative roles. We do that work when it comes to us, but we are not here for that.

What is administration? My own understanding of this form of work relies on something like a base/superstructure model. I visualize universities as comprising two zones of activity that are at once profoundly different and separate and profoundly interdependent. In one of these, the activities that are the purpose of the university take place: study, reflection, discussion, the transmission of knowledge and the interrogation of received ideas, and the building of bonds between people from different backgrounds who are engaged in these common pursuits. (This formulation is of course very approximate.) These activities are in essence intellectual, one might even say ideal. But it is their peculiarity that they require support from another sphere of activity that is the reverse of ideal: practical, bureaucratic, material or physical, economic. So a course is, in its moments of intense self-realization, a wholly intellectual transaction, a vivid sharing and questioning of knowledge performed together by teacher and student. But in another, just-as-real sense, a course is the set of not-in-the-least intellectual arrangements that made this intellectual experience possible: it meets at an hour that has to be arranged, in a location that has to be arranged, in a building whose physical maintenance has to be arranged, led by an instructor who has to be hired, whose qualifications have to be approved, whose parking space has to be arranged, whose benefits and salary have to be arranged, working with students who have to be selectively admitted according to policies and procedures that have to be arranged, who themselves require study space, and residential space, and dining hall menus, all of which require to be arranged, and . . . you get the idea.

The educational operations of a university are not reducible to its bureaucratic arrangements, but they can't take place separate from those arrangements. Those arrangements create the possibility of an experience of a different order, an experience free to forget the arrangements that provided its occasion — what is called the life of the mind. This, I take it, is what administration is in a university: a temporary crossing over from the realm of education proper into the enabling realm of arrangement. It follows that good administration isn't just the art of skillful management, but is that practice of management that retains a powerful sense of what it is trying to enable, what nonpractical goal it is trying to ad-minister or minister to. (My Latin dictionary gives these senses for the noun *administer, administri:* servant, underling, assistant, agent, attendant, priest.)

All of which is true enough, but fails to capture the drama that can attach to administration. This arises from the fact that arrangement and management require choices, choices to be made in the midst of competing communal preferences and with finite resources for their realization. A stupid joke of my youth ran: "Would you like to go to California or by bus?" But just this absurd asymmetry characterizes the kinds of choices that come up in the zone of administration. Would you rather subscribe to obscure periodicals for the library — since who knows what apparently minor periodical in what apparently marginal language will turn out to be considered a major cultural document? — or put a roof on a severely leaky lab? Would you rather paint the admissions office — an educational issue, since appearances can affect matriculation and Yale wants to draw the best — or hire extra teaching assistants for an over-crowded course? Would you do better to try to upgrade athletic facilities or career counseling services? Support new interdisciplinary programs or fix more antiquated bathrooms?

Such choices in reality come up not in pairs but as the rivalry of each desirable thing against every other one. Each claim comes with direct educational benefits if adopted and possibly dire consequences if neglected. At the same time, when decisions must be made, there's no knowing for sure which choice will prove to have been the best or wisest—only the certainty of displeasing those who counseled on the other side. Trying to make intelligent choices while working in this particular darkness is the fun of administration.

Two things help here. First, administration at Yale is a highly collegial affair. Almost nothing at Yale has ever been accomplished autocratically. Successful management has instead involved large amounts of consultation with faculty, students, staff, and administrative colleagues, so that none of us moves forward with our own unaided light. Second, the academic culture of Yale puts a much lower premium on administrative affairs than it does on intellectual ones. Yale is sometimes inefficient as a result, but the healthy consequence is that Yale tends not to forget what management is in the service of—what educational goals bureaucracy is trying to effect.

In these conditions, I'm happy to make a temporary deviation into the administrative zone. Having a job like my current one is the only way to get a sense of how the whole of Yale works. So I greet it as a new phase of my education—and after I've done it for a while, it'll be someone else's turn, and I'll cross back into my more usual habitat.

AN ANATOMY OF
MULTICULTURALISM

This essay, which began life as a talk to alumni, was written in the heyday of the so-called Culture Wars in the early 1990s. It reflects my view that the basis of that once-famous conflict, the polemical war between Western Civilization–based curricula and their modern antitheses, represented a false choice and an impoverished model of education. First published in the *Yale Alumni Magazine*, April 1994.

THERE ONCE WAS a time when literate culture—the things educated people know and believe other people should know—possessed certain well-marked features. The contents of literate culture were internally coherent; they were widely agreed to; and above all they were agreed to be universal in their interest or meaning. What happened in education, according to this understanding, was that we came out of whatever local, parochial origin we happened to have been born in to meet on the ground of the universally significant. In literature, we studied the work not of those who expressed themselves "like us" but of writers who transcended such limits of time and place—writers with names like Homer and Shakespeare. In philosophy we read not those who thought the way people think where we came from but thinkers of perennial, transcultural significance: Plato, for instance, or Rousseau.

A current caricature says that this model of education was only ever subscribed to by the elite, but historically this is quite untrue. During its long reign the concept of universal culture was often valued especially highly by outsiders. When W. E. B. DuBois, the great African-American intellectual of the turn of the 19th century, looked for an image of a profound human unity to set against the racial segregations being perfected in his time, he turned to the literary classics: "I sit with Shakespeare and he winces not," he wrote in *The Souls of Black Folk* (1903). You would recoil if I sat next to you at the whites-only lunch counter, DuBois implies, but Shakespeare doesn't when I sit and read his plays. For DuBois, culture restores the common ground that local social arrangements deny.

The educational revolution for which multiculturalism is a shorthand name embodies an unraveling of this older consensus. Multiculturalism has arisen through the spreading of the idea that the so-called universal was in fact only partial: one side of the story pretending to be the whole story, the interests of some groups passing themselves off as the interests of all. "Tonto! Tonto! We are surrounded by Indians!" the Lone Ranger said in an old joke; and like Tonto, many contemporary readers have come to respond: "What do you mean 'we'?" So a line like "The *Odyssey* exemplifies the fundamental human desire to wander and adventure," a classroom truism not long ago, would now provoke the quick retort: "'Human' to be sure, if humans are assumed to be men. But what about that wife who sat home while Odysseus got to wander?"

In recent years the growing suspicion of alleged universals has led to a heightened sense that there are always many parties to every human experience, and that their experiences of the same event are often profoundly divergent. In the wake of this realization, it has come to seem that real education is to be found not in the move from the local to the generalizedly "human" but in the effort to hear and attend to all the different voices of human history—the voices of those who have dominated the official stories, but also those silenced or minimized by the official account. We know we are in the neighborhood of this new plan of education whenever history is given us in plural, contending versions: when the story of *The Odyssey* is also considered from Penelope's point of view; when Columbus's discovery of America is seen not just from the European but also from the Arawak or Taino vantage; when the history of the Pilgrim settlement takes into account the different history it produced for native populations; and so on.

We have all seen the profound educational shift that has taken place in this country as the second of these models has begun to displace the first in recent years. Having been taught in the older of these ways, but lived to teach and be reeducated in the newer one, I have had, by pure historical coincidence, an intimate experience of this great tectonic shift. Here I offer a few reflections on how this still-unfolding revolution looks to a person who has seen it from both sides.

There are, in truth, a great many things to say about this transformation. The first and most obvious is that it embodies a playing out in education of a contemporary social drama that ranges far beyond the sphere of education itself. When our successors look back on the second half of this century, the Civil Rights movement will surely strike them as one of the most decisive developments in the history of our time. As we know, this movement led a nation that had accepted legal segregation to become first embarrassed by, then to seek to reform, the practice of discrimination based on race. Having begun with this focus, the Civil Rights movement has extended itself by the force of analogy, creating the perception that many other forms of social differentiation—the different treatment of women, of other minorities, of the disabled, and so on—were as unjust and unjustifiable as racial discrimination. The modern sentiment that men and women should win advancement only on the grounds of individual ability, and not because of the groups they can be lumped into, has made for changes in college admissions, corporate hiring, professional recruitment, and virtually every other social practice in the United States. In the world of education, it has expressed itself as multiculturalism. Multiculturalism embodies the ideal of equal opportunity implemented at the level of the curriculum—the urge to open the field of study, like other places of visibility and prestige, to women, minorities, and others previously left out of account.

To its partisans, multicultural education is a matter of justice done at last. But there are many who are in sympathy with these social goals who still regard their educational effects as pernicious. One common cry is that this movement's political ends are leading it to abandon a long-cherished heritage education has passed down from generation to generation. But to this it can be replied that the history of education is a history of change more than any of us likes to admit. We all tend to share the sense that the things we studied in school had probably been taught there since time immemorial, and so should continue to be taught until the end of time. But our schoolings were themselves often products of reforms that had succeeded and then been forgotten. What subject could seem more timeless than English? But English wasn't thought a fit matter for university study before the 19th century: it was a modern, vernacular literature, and education's business was with the Classical. My own field, American literature, entered college curricula later still, not much earlier than 1940, having been dismissed as a mere colonial appendage of English after English got itself academically accepted. "What . . . at one time has been held in little estimation, and has hardly found place in a course in liberal instruction, has, under other circumstances, risen to repute, and received a proportional share of attention," President Jeremiah Day wrote in the Yale Report of 1828. Seen against such a background, it may be possible to regard current curricular revolutions as the latest chapter of a long story of change, not an unprecedented deviance saved for modern times.

But the central objection to multicultural reforms comes from the belief that traditional literate culture is more meaningful than newly promoted objects of study—that the lives and works of the hitherto ignored, however much we may wish to feature them for sentimental or political reasons, are less remarkable human achievements than the classics, and their study therefore less rewarding. (Saul Bellow meant this when he asked: "Where is the Zulu Tolstoy?") This is a weighty charge, but to it we might reply: How could you know that these things are less valuable except by having studied them, extended them your sympathy, and given them your patient attention? A silent premise of much of my education was that there were all manner of things not worth knowing about and that we could know they were not worth knowing without bothering to consult them. When I came to the study of American literature, for example, I often read that Hawthorne, Melville, and the other geniuses of the American Renaissance wrote in opposition to a popular sentimental literature of unimaginable banality, and — in a beautiful convenience — my contemporaries and I understood that there was no need to read this work in order to be confident of its perfect worthlessness. From a later vantage I can testify that when one takes the trouble to look into them, ignored or downvalued traditions — even the mid-19th-century sentimental novel — can turn out to contain creations of extraordinary power and interest. (There would be no need to make this point for our own time, when the achievements of women and minorities are unmistakable; what contemporary literature course would leave out such great American writers as the Asian-American Maxine Hong Kingston, or the African-American Toni Morrison, or the Mexican-American Richard Rodriguez?) My own career in the last 15 years had led me to be increasingly engaged with writers from outside the traditional canon. In my courses I now frequently teach authors from hitherto ignored traditions together with their more famous contemporaries — Frederick Douglass and Fanny Fern with Herman Melville, Louisa May Alcott and Charles W. Chesnutt with Mark Twain. And in my classes such writers do not just add new material, they substantially change and enrich the terms on which every author is grasped and understood.

In my experience then, without causing any defection from the classic authors I still love, teach, and value, the changes associated with multiculturalism have brought a real renovation, a widening of the field of knowledge and a deepened understanding of everything it contains. Yet without in any way retracting what I have said, it seems to me possible to wonder whether current ways of conceptualizing and implementing multicultural education are as problem-free as some proponents imply. If the older model of education had its limits, the new program has a potential to enmesh us in limits of its own; and a full assessment would want to reckon these dangers together with the advantages it might supply.

To mention three problems very quickly: Multiculturalism has promoted an inclusionistic curriculum. Its moral imperative not to discriminate leads it to want to put everything in and leave nothing out. But there is an undeniable danger that the practice of universal curricular representation can degenerate into high-minded tokenism. Everyone has seen the new-style school anthologies and curricular units with snippet samplings of all the nation's or world's peoples. Like all official school instruments, these show the strong sense of feeling answerable to a vigilant cultural authority that watches their every move. The old-style textbook paid obeisance to an imaginary censor who asked: "Are we being sufficiently patriotic? Are we avoiding blasphemy and smut?" The new one's choices show it similarly attentive to a moral overseer who asks, for instance: "Have we got our Native American? Our Asian-American? Is our black a man? If so, have we also got a black woman?"

I mean no denigration of these groups when I say that a curriculum composed by checking off the proper inclusion of such groups often results in tokenistic representation, and, worse, in what I'd call "Epcotization": the reproduction of complicated cultural experiences into so many little manageable units, pleasurably foreign yet quickly consumable, that we can wheel in and out of at high velocity and leave with a complacent sense that we have now appreciated that. To my mind, it would be not a hater but a lover of serious multiculturalism who would feel that much contemporary multicultural education teaches naive, presumptuous attitudes toward the cultures it intends to honor. A week on Rudolfo Anaya's *Bless Me, Ultima* or Chinua Achebe's *Things Fall Apart* in the well-meaning modern classroom and the mysteries of Chicano or African life seem to lie revealed! But I would have thought that one of the first points we would want to learn about other people is that their lives are not so easily known, and that their cultures exist not to display their beauties to outsiders but in part to protect them against such intrusions. As the benevolent study of other cultures gets more deeply installed in the earliest levels of education I can imagine the objects of multicultural appreciation rising up against their appreciators to say: "Recognize our reality, yes, but stop thinking you can know us so easily." Such a reply has already been heard from the Native American woman who wrote to the *New York Times* to ask, in response to an article on a California grade-school curriculum in which children learned to perform mini-versions of tribal rituals, how they would like it if their children were taught how to perform the crucifixion with popsicle sticks? Zora Neale Hurston, the great novelist of the Harlem Renaissance, wrote this warning against the presumptions of culture-crossing in her ethnological study *Mules and Men* (1936): "The theory behind our [i.e., African-American] tactics: 'The white man is always trying to know somebody else's business. All right, I'll set something outside the door of my mind for him to play with and handle. He can read my writing but he sho' can't read my mind.'"

In a parallel naivete, the "It's a Small World" or "Rainbow Curriculum" tends to put forth an Edward Hicks model of cultural relations, displaying a peaceable kingdom where the lion lies down with the lamb and every other beast. But this humane image conceals the lesson that the relations among cultures tend quite as often to conflict as to complementarity. I remember a colleague of mine coming back from a year in Berlin to report how mystified European academics were by the American desire to teach all our separate traditions in place of a unified, common culture. In the vicinity of Eastern Europe, he said, such a presentation would be a reminder of ethnic conflicts always threatening to erupt into violence. This was in 1988, on the eve of the Yugoslavian civil war.

In addition to these potentials for naivete, a second danger of modern multiculturalism lies in the tendency to confer a dubious absoluteness on group identities and group labels.

Some parts of American society are experiencing a kind of romance of gender and ethnicity at present, in which an alluring aura comes to surround an object to the extent that that it can be found to derive from a formerly marginalized group. Through this familiar logic, a book like Forrest Carter's *The Education of Little Tree* won wide adoption as a high and junior high school text in part because its author was understood to be an Indian (it has since been learned that he was a white segregationist); and even so powerful a book as Hurston's *Their Eyes Were Watching God* has received a curricular exposure out of all proportion to its interest because its author fit the double categories Woman and Black. (For Hurston's ironic reflections on such an abstraction or generalization of her meaning, read her essay "How It Feels To Be Colored Me.")

To practice this kind of extrapolation from the person to the category catches a valuable half-truth, namely that none of us is only individual, and all of us have had our individual lives shaped by the social positions we have lived in. At the same time, a perpetual and un-self-critical practice of extrapolation from person to category negates the countervailing truth — that no human group is homogeneous, and that no person has his or her identity set solely by the groups he or she belongs to. When we teach the habit of thinking of people as Men and Women and Whites and Blacks, we run the risk of teaching — without meaning to — that people can be adequately identified by such generalizing labels. But this way danger lies, for what made the multicultural revolution necessary in the first place was the existence of a world where qualified people could be denied places in schools because they were blacks, or because they were women, and so on.

Last, just to the extent that they value the enrichment it supplies, proponents of multiculturalism will want to protect against another lurking danger: the presumption that its contributions have a monopoly on everything important to know. Occasionally one meets people for whom multiculturalism means not the amplification of a knowledge now found incomplete but the notion that what has heretofore been ignored is valuable, and what has hitherto been valued is pernicious, part of a conspiracy of dehumanization and oppression. I confess that I have met products of recent education who knew the new pan-ethnic literary canon to perfection but who were ignorant of great traditional authors and content to be so; people who had subtle thoughts about (for instance) Nella Larsen's recently rediscovered novel *Passing* but who took no interest in Faulkner's nearly contemporary novel of racial passing, *Light in August*, since Faulkner was a famous misogynist.

What is this attitude? A new manifestation, surely, of the same presumption I mocked in multiculturalism's more traditionalist foes, the presumption that what I already know and like is worth knowing, and what I don't is fit to ignore. But no educational program can contain the whole of wisdom. Every educational model closed-mindedly embraced can be made a home for prejudice and self-limitation, the new as much as the old. Multiculturalism's great achievement was to teach us that traditional literate culture did not include everything worth knowing, and that the right corrective for its limits was to reach outside its boundaries and learn to appreciate the different things encountered there. But multicultural education will do itself a favor if it remembers to apply this same lesson to itself: to be aware of the boundaries its own enthusiasms establish, and to strive to feel the power of things outside its ken – the works of traditional culture not least. (And there are still plenty of world cultures that are not registered with any detail or seriousness even in "reformed" American education.)

The current revolution in education has opened our eyes to many worlds of human experience that lie outside of received accounts. In so doing, it has produced an enormous enrichment and made school an exciting place. But what multiculturalism is not is an all-purpose solution to the problem of education. Like all educational programs, it has things it can teach us, and like all programs it will enforce its inevitable limits on us if we do not take pains to avoid them. That said, it seems to me that the major challenge for thoughtful education now is neither to try to prevent the multicultural revolution nor simply to help install it in power. Rather, it is to subject this program to the fullest possible exercise of intelligence, imagination, curiosity, and self-criticism, so that as we add its contributions to the field of knowledge, we maximally realize its powers of extension—and maximally protect ourselves from its powers of limitation.

ON RESIDENTIAL EDUCATION

An example of the occasional editorials I wrote as Dean on campus issues, this was sparked by a widespread student move off campus that threatened significant impairment to the Yale residential college experience. In college, decisions about where students will live are also decisions about whom they will know and what they will teach each other. First printed in the *Yale Daily News*, March 21, 1995.

I AGREE AS a general thing that administrators should be seen and not heard, but occasionally an issue arises so central to our life together that it seems wrong for the Dean to hold his peace.

But having summoned my nerve and edged forward to speak, I find that I lack a channel, an organized means of public address. With thanks to the editors, I here avail myself of the opinion-molding powers of the daily press. Heed my words or I may have to resort to heavier weaponry: talk radio?

The time of year is here for choosing whether to live on campus or off. I write to urge anyone thinking of moving off campus to think again.

My current job has made me a significant expert in the reasons for moving off campus. I have learned of the existential necessity for more space than college rooms afford. I have heard the argument for more privacy; for less noise; for a more personalized diet; for tastier, better prepared, and cheaper food, such as is apparently invariably supplied by one's own and one's friends' cuisine; for cleaner bathrooms and better maintenance (I rejoice in the notion of Yale students as frustrated good housekeepers); and for the right to live with one's particular pals in flexibly sized configurations.

And, though few people have put it to me in these terms, I also understand the argument for adulthood. Having one's own apartment, buying one's own groceries, doing one's own dishes — everyone who has done these things for the first time knows the satisfactions they carry as emblems of independence achieved at last.

I in no way minimize the force of these arguments. Nor would I deny that they include legitimate criticisms of campus living conditions that the University must seriously address. But even if all the contra arguments were conceded — even if the absolute worst "take" on college living were accepted and the absolute brightest picture of life off campus were taken for true (this would of course be a most naive position) — there would still be significant claims for living "on" that this reasoning would badly underrate.

The romance of independent living will not last forever. I promise you that your later life will not be deficient in chances to cook your own meals, do your own dishes, and clean your own bathroom — events that will not always retain their initial charm. When it fades into a chronic condition, independent living will reveal that it has limits bound together with its pleasures — limits strongly connected to some general woes of our culture.

Apartment living yields the good of privacy at the price of connecting living to apartness, to social separation and self-enclosure. Generalized, this model looks forward to something the modern American world knows much too much of: the withdrawal into private spaces, into so many separate dwellings where a small group of associates gathers around its centers of private entertainment, with a corresponding impoverishment of the sense of public, communal life.

Living with one's very best friends, similarly, is the happy name for a fact that takes on quite different meanings when practiced on a large scale. Especially in the era of suburbanization, modern America has seen a growth of spatial separations in which people choose to live close together with people "like" themselves and out of sight of people of different incomes, origins, customs, and traditions. Whether this trend has yielded the richest experience of humanity, and whether it has improved our ability to work together to envision a satisfactory collective world, I leave it to you to decide.

It is against the background of these developments that Yale's residential colleges carry, in my view, their moral meaning. In the colleges Yalies have available something that later life, whatever its freedoms and advantages, will make hard indeed to obtain: a chance to live as a member of a community; to have easy, daily contact with representatives of every part of our world; the chance to learn how to live together, to enjoy together, and to work together to realize the best possibilities of associated life.

The University has work to do on its side. Extensive efforts are now under way to improve the physical conditions of the colleges and to bring college dining into higher favor. Improved computer services for all college rooms will soon be announced. While college housing will never be palatial, we must do everything we can to guarantee a decent, comfortable level of on-campus accommodation.

But while students are quite right to insist on an appropriate level of comfort, I trust they will not be so short-sighted as to make this the sole factor in deciding where and how to live. Anyone who lives on campus can tell you: there are costs to living in the college, costs of space, of privacy, and more. But living in maximum comfort has its costs as well — real costs in social experience, a costly self-distancing from the full Yale scene.

Students of Yale College, heed your Dean! Come join the Yale community, pitch in and help make it flourish. This is one of the great educations Yale has to offer you. If you are resolved to look elsewhere, that is fine too. But please make sure you have taken the full measure of what you might be giving up.

ON SEXUAL HARASSMENT

Few issues are more vexed in the modern university than that of romantic relations between teachers and students. This editorial tries to express the moral complexity of the issue while arguing for a change in university policy. The proposed change was later enacted. *Yale Daily News*, December 5, 1996.

I HAVE WRITTEN the Provost to request a reconsideration of the policy on sexual harassment as outlined in the Faculty Handbook.

Yale's policy is unambiguous in stating that "sexual harassment is antithetical to academic values and to a work environment free from the fact or appearance of coercion." This is as it should be. Sexual harassment represents a serious misapplication of the power a teacher has over a student. It introduces altogether inappropriate dimensions into the pedagogical relationship, skewing the essential activities of evaluation, advising, and so on. For this reason, our commitment as educators must lead us to condemn sexual harassment not just as generally unethical but as a perversion of the university's central functions, teaching and learning. The language of existing policy makes this point clearly enough.

Where our stated policy is less than adequate, in my opinion, is in the language governing quasi-consensual relations between teacher and student. The Faculty Handbook avoids forbidding such relations while also underlining that the inequality inherent in such relations gives them a latent quality of potential coerciveness—a coerciveness which, if complained of afterward, can sustain a charge of sexual harassment even in a relation "apparently founded on mutual consent." In the language of the Handbook, "Because of the special trust and the inequality of status inherent in the teacher-student relationship, sexual relations between a teacher and his or her student, even when apparently founded on mutual consent, are potentially coercive, and may be so regarded if a complaint of sexual harassment arises."

I can imagine the reasoning that lay behind this phrasing. The happy, long-lasting, and productive unions that exist between some professors and their former students makes it seem a little facile to denounce all such relations as prima facie immoral. Yale's existing policy tries to find a difficult balance between recognizing the dangers hidden in such relations and a countervailing principle that is also of high value in the university – the right of adults to make their own choices and to take responsibility for the consequences of their choices with a minimum of institutional interference.

But while I am as reluctant as anyone to infringe on this freedom, and while I respect the Handbook's effort to deal with the moral complexities of an issue whose difficulties are not always acknowledged, the policy that results from this balancing act has clear incongruities. If apparent consent cannot free a relationship of latent coercion, then consent itself, it would seem, is not the real issue: at bottom our policy implies that the asymmetry of authority between teacher and student makes in inappropriate for teachers to subject students to sexual attentions however those attentions are received. Further, if we are willing to uphold a charge of harassment made retrospectively where harassment was not seen initially, then it seems simply mistaken to imply that sexual relations between teacher and student can be even provisionally allowed. Do it if you must, but at the peril of retrospective revisionism, we now caution – but if the teacher's actions can be judged wrong in hindsight, then perhaps we ought to say up front: Just don't. Having sexual relations with one's students is just not something teachers should do.

Policy changes won't save us from the difficulties that actual cases of sexual harassment will present us with. However clear our official language, charges of sexual harassment cannot be sustained without appropriate evidence, which in this domain will often prove quite murky. When an offense has been determined, finding a punishment that fits the offense will not always be easy either, and may sometimes require agonizing decisions among imperfectly appropriate alternatives.

But in an area that can't be entirely rescued from the ambiguities of human nature and human conduct, the least we can do is to give as clear a message as we can about the university's expectations. It is in this spirit that I have requested a reconsideration of our policy.

TWO WRITERS' BEGINNINGS

EUDORA WELTY IN THE NEIGHBORHOOD
OF RICHARD WRIGHT

A selection from the scholarly work I composed while Dean, this essay engages an issue at the heart of that role's concerns: how education shapes continuing understandings and social roles. Reprinted from *The Yale Review*, April 1996.

THE PUBLICATION of Eudora Welty's *One Writer's Beginnings* in 1984 was a surprise in several ways. This book represented, first, a breaking of a fairly prolonged silence. Although Welty had published her selected essays in 1978 and her collected stories in 1980, no wholly new work had appeared since *The Optimist's Daughter* in 1972, and Welty had seemed comfortably settled into the final phase of a certain sort of literary life: collecting honors and prizes for lifetime achievement, good-naturedly personifying the distinguished author on public occasions, sometimes reading from her beloved stories but no longer pretending to produce. At the same time that it showed that her authorship was still alive, this book also featured Welty turning to a new and unexpected mode of creation. The most modest major writer of her generation, Welty had made a career of professing that everything was more interesting than herself and that writing existed to carry the writer *out* of herself. *One Writer's Beginnings* is no work of hot confession, but it embodies a clear effort to work against Welty's own long-established grain: to explore in public the terms of her personal life.

But for those who follow stories of authors and their emergence, *One Writer's Beginnings* carried a further surprise of which its author was almost certainly unaware, in its revelation that not one but two writers began from the same point of origin. Richard Wright's *Black Boy,* a book lopped off from a longer memoir by Wright's editors to fit it for Book-of-the-Month Club adoption, was a major best-seller when it was published in 1945, and it has since enjoyed the status of a classic African-American autobiography. What Welty's volume invited readers to recognize was that these authors were in some sense a twinned birth, for all their differences—indeed just *in* their differences—joint products of a shared social sense.

It is incongruous to think of Wright and Welty together. The versions of authorship these two projected are so symmetrically opposed as to make them seem like each other's photographic negative: Wright, so emphatically the author as black man, Welty no less unmistakably the writer as (white) lady; his the authorship always of rage, hers of complex graces and controlled modulations of tone; he the laureate of the psychic tolls of organized public racism, she the explorer of the private realms of self-enclosed subjectivity and family life; Wright, the author faulted by his protégé James Baldwin for writing protest fiction, fiction too overtly infused with political intent; Welty, the writer chided during the Civil Rights movement for the apolitical quality of her art, a stance she defended in the highwater year of the Great Society in the defensive essay "Must the Novelist Crusade?" Antitheses to the outside eye, Wright and Welty also failed to seize any occasion to think of themselves as related. Michel Fabre's densely detailed biography of Wright contains no mention of Welty in its six hundred long pages. In *Conversations with Eudora Welty,* Peggy Whitman Prenshaw's compilation of interviews published over forty years, interlocutors several times bring up Wright's name to Welty, and each time Welty refuses to take them up on the invitation to discuss him.

But if this comparison is unobvious, once it occurs to us to make it, strange symmetries reveal themselves between Welty and Wright. They emerged to public notice in exactly the same late Depression/eve of World War II years, Wright with *Uncle Tom's Children* (1938) and *Native Son* (1941), Welty with *A Curtain of Green* (1941) and *The Robber Bridegroom* (1942). They won similar—sometimes identical—recognitions on their emergence: Wright won a Guggenheim Fellowship in 1939, Welty in 1942; Wright won the O. Henry Award for "Fire and Cloud" and "Almos' a Man" in 1938 and 1940, Welty won the same award for "A Worn Path" and "The Wide Net" in 1941 and 1942. Before committing themselves to literary careers, Wright and Welty both worked for the Works Progress Administration in the mid-1930s, she as a publicity agent in Mississippi, he as a researcher in Chicago. From within this early shelter, the Depression's great gift to American artists, Wright had turned from his first genre—leftist poetry—to fiction writing in 1935. Welty made the same turn from her first genre, photography, in the same year.

Such coincidences mark Wright and Welty as joint exploiters of the circumstances of authorship in the late-1930s—early-1940s United States. What *One Writer's Beginnings* shows is that if we press farther back in their careers, these coincidences begin to transform themselves from chance likenesses into a real convergence. For Welty's memoir reminds us that these two writers were born within seven months of each other (he in September 1908, she in April 1909) in the same state and, more critically, that they lived in the same town—Jackson, Mississippi—from ages ten to seventeen, the years they make the focal point of their works of reminiscence. Nothing can establish that the young Wright and Welty ever knew of each other, as they almost certainly did not. But because they lived together in a town of twenty thousand—a town "so small," as Welty later remembered it, "that one knew everybody practically"—it seems wholly likely that they would have laid eyes on each other, that even if without recognizing it they formed part of each other's daily world or visual field. Once we begin thinking of each in terms of the parallel life of the other, Wright's and Welty's biographies become shrouded with a haunting sense of proximity: an excruciating sense of the extreme physical closeness, to each, of the very differently composed life of the other, and of the deep familiarity they would have shared, if on different terms, with the spaces of a common world.

Thought of as fellow citizens or unconscious neighbors, every scene in one's biography becomes a place to note the possible presence, absence, or distanced nearness of the other. Welty's father worked on Capitol Street, the chief commercial street of Jackson, and she remembers visiting his office after Sunday School. The black boy Richard Wright did not visit Christian Welty at Lamar Life and would hardly have been welcome to, but in a manuscript passage later cut from *Black Boy,* Wright remembers shopping with his grandmother on this same street, while white shoppers (Chestina Welty and her children?) stare at this white-looking woman with two black children in tow. (*Black Boy* positions Wright's job as a bellboy at the Edwards Hotel as a major scene of his education into the stunting rules of segregationist self-subordination. The Edwards Hotel was also on Capitol Street, an easy walk from Lamar Life.) In *One Writer's Beginnings,* Welty remembers early silent movies, then a new cultural presence, as a great entertainment of her youth, and she recalls watching the Keystone Kops and *The Cabinet of Doctor Caligari* "on the screen of the Istrione Theater (known as the Eyestrain)." A map of Jackson will show that the Istrione Theater was on Capitol Street near the corner of Farish, the principal black business street of Jackson. In a famous episode in *Black Boy,* young Richard participates in a ticket-selling scam at a contemporaneous movie theater open to blacks. Fabre identifies this as the Alamo Theater on Amite Street, one block away from the Istrione: so close are their parallel worlds.

The interest of putting Wright and Welty back into the margins of each other's stories goes beyond the pleasures of literary coincidence. I take the conjunction of Wright's and Welty's lives in Jackson between 1918 and 1925 to exemplify, in the most localized and concrete way, a more general fact and enigma of American cultural history. It has often been noticed that the South, exactly in the period when it stood as the most backward region of the United States, was a particularly prolific source of American literary talent. (In addition to Welty and Wright, in the earlier twentieth century Mississippi alone gave American literature such major figures as William Faulkner and Tennessee Williams.) But the how and why of this process have remained mysterious. Likely-sounding suggestions have been made as to why the South should have been such a breeding ground of writers—the South, having lost the war, knew the inspirations of poverty and tragedy, not the stultifications of success and material prosperity; the South, by being behindhand at modernization, retained a lively oral storytelling tradition—but anyone who has tried to connect such theories to the particulars of individual authors' emergence will have recognized the extreme weakness of their explanatory power. Mysteriously prolific of authors, the South between the Civil War and integration or Second Reconstruction also fed not one "Southern" tradition but the profoundly different traditions of mainstream and African-American letters. One South was the home to Mark Twain and Charles W. Chesnutt, William Faulkner and Zora Neale Hurston, Welty and Wright, Ralph Ellison and Flannery O'Connor; but how one place could have stimulated disjunctive modes of creation is also imperfectly understood. As I read it, Welty's and Wright's shared life gives us a case for the study of these related mysteries. My project here is to rejoin these habitually separated authors and to think them back onto a unified social ground; then to watch how their experiences of that common origin propelled them on their different literary paths.

We might begin this conjunctive history by noting that the place these authors cohabited was not just Anytown. Jackson was the capital city of a state that had a particularly salient identity in Wright and Welty's youth. The historian of Mississippi John Ray Skates writes:

> In the 1920s, Mississippi was a forgotten state in a forgotten region. Nationally, the 1920s are usually described as the "roaring twenties." Mississippi hardly roared. Americans in the 1920s were more prosperous than ever before in the nation's history. Mississippians were poor. At a time when material comfort through the mass production of consumer

goods became almost a national religion, Mississippians found themselves left out. With a per-capita income of $396, only one-third of the national average, Mississippians little understood the moral arguments of the 1920s over America's worship of material things. The United States in the 1920s had already become an urban nation. The glamorous, growing cities were the magnet of the nation, attracting the bright and ambitious. America's cities in the 1920s became the country's newest frontier. Mississippi, meanwhile, remained over-whelmingly rural. In 1920, 86.6 percent of the state's citizens lived in the country. . . . Nor did the great social questions of the decade seem to affect Mississippi. Restriction of immigra-tion could hardly be of much interest in a state whose popula-tion was almost wholly native-born.

Skates does not mention the racial system that accompa-nied Mississippi's early-twentieth-century poverty, but Jackson was also a capital seat of state-mandated segregation and the racist mindset that attended it. Though other states held this dubious honor in the first years of official segregation, in the early twentieth century Mississippi took on the distinction of providing the leading advocates of white supremacy. Two of the most famous were notably associated with Jackson in the years under discussion: James K. Vardaman, who presided as Gover-nor in the statehouse two blocks down Eudora Welty's street before going on to the Senate (it was Vardaman who said, "The way to control the nigger is to whip him when he does not obey without it"), and the egregious Theodore G. Bilbo, in Wright's and Welty's childhoods a State Senator, then Lieutenant Gover-nor, then Governor of Mississippi.

But to think of Jackson only as the capital of these retro-grade developments is to miss an important part of the story. For the same city that gave political focus and legal fixity to Mississippi racism was itself changing in the years of Wright's and Welty's childhoods, in ways that—without altering the rule of racial segregation—brought Jackson into closer touch with trans–Southern American development. The fascinating *Missis-sippi: A Guide to the Magnolia State* (1938), part of the state guide series produced by the Federal Writers' Project of the WPA, reports of Jackson that "in a State that is predominantly rural, it alone has the metropolitan touch," and it was during the years under discussion that this touch was effected. The population boomed in this period: a small town indeed at the start, Jackson's population tripled, from 7,800 to 21,300, between 1900 and 1910, and after holding steady again doubled, from 22,800 to 48,000, between 1920 and 1930. Driving this growth was a rapid expansion in the government, industrial, and service sectors of the Jackson economy, developments that gave it more connection to contemporaneous national evolutions and that increasingly differentiated it from the cotton- and lumber-dependent economies of the rest of the state. These new sources of economic opportunity made Jackson itself, in Skates's apt word, an urban magnet in the early twentieth century, and as its population and wealth grew, Jackson became conspicuously more modern, generating the sort of civic features that marked the up-to-date contemporary city. These include cultural structures like the Carnegie Library (1914) and the Civic Auditorium (1923); tall, skyline-dominating commercial buildings (Jackson's first, the Lamar Life home office — just like in *Oklahoma!* a skyscraper seven stories high — was completed in 1925); and a modernized public school system. Jackson's Central High School, one of the first in the state, became fully accredited in 1921. In the same year Jackson opened its first differentiated junior high school, described by Jackson school historian William Dalehite as "the most modern of its day with a cafeteria, domestic science department, manual training, a library, and specially equipped science rooms."

Remembering this history of modernization and development is critical for understanding Eudora Welty's and Richard Wright's beginnings, for neither lived in Jackson as an old settler. Both came to Jackson through the action of these larger social processes, and their lives were in every way shaped by these transformations.

Although Welty does not underline the fact, the childhood landscape she sketches in *One Writer's Beginnings* was a landscape of institutions and structures quite new when she encountered them. Her grade school, the fondly remembered Jefferson Davis Grammar School, was built within three years of her birth. (Welty graduated from Central High in 1925, four years after the school's accreditation.) The Carnegie Library she remembers precociously using opened only when she was six. Her father supervised the building of Lamar Life's new corporate headquarters, which she recalls being allowed to climb up, on the fire escape, before it was completed.

In fact, Welty's presence in Jackson is inexplicable without reference to these larger patterns of change. Perhaps the greatest surprise in *One Writer's Beginnings* is the revelation that Eudora Welty, *echt* Southern writer and chief celebrant of local attachments, was a relative newcomer to Mississippi. Late in the book we learn that Welty's parents were voluntary Southerners, having elected to move from their childhood homes on the Ohio–West Virginia border when they married and having chosen Welty's apparently inevitable hometown over a once equally plausible alternative, the Thousand Islands in upstate New York. Welty rather strikingly fails to comment either on the manifest difference between these choices (a Southern friend has likened it to a choice between moving to Sweden or South Africa) or on the thought-process that informed her parents' decision. Her mother, she notes, made the decision between alternatives proposed by her father, and a comment in an interview of 1981 on her mother's regional sympathies — "she was from Virginia stock on both sides. She considered herself a Southerner of the first water" — may supply the lost logic of this choice. But it seems at least as likely that Christian Welty spotted better opportunities in Jackson when he scouted these alternatives, opportunities intimately tied to accelerating economic development. The Lamar Mutual Life Insurance Company, founded in reaction against the high premiums charged in the South by out-of-region companies, was a new enterprise in 1906, a perfect example of the growth of indigenous industries in Jackson at this time. Christian Welty found his opportunity in this expansion: he came to Jackson as a bookkeeper for the new company, was soon (Welty reports) "made secretary and one of the directors," and rose to the presidency of the company before his death in 1931. Welty was in this strict sense supported by Jackson's new economic development, living in the new world — or one of the new worlds — that it created: the world, then common enough in the North but rare and emergent in early-1900s Mississippi, of white-collar fathers and managerial-professional-class customs and attitudes. (As president of the Garden Club, Welty's mother helped mastermind the planting of the seven thousand crepe myrtles hailed by the WPA guide as "Jackson's loveliest natural attraction.")

Behind Welty's family history we can detect the workings of that uneven, protracted historical process usually called the Birth of the New South. Richard Wright lived on the other side of town from Welty, but he, too, came to Jackson through a process of mobility, and in his case, too, this mobility has both a local family logic and a larger historical resonance. The larger resonance is with what historians call the Great Migration: the mass movement, spurred by the failure of the cotton economy at one end and the growth of industrial opportunity at the other, that led 1.2 million blacks to leave the South for Northern cities between 1916 and 1927 alone. As has long been recognized, Wright's life — he was born to a sharecropper on a former plantation — enacts the classic move from the rural South to the urban North and its growing ghettos, the move he is poised to make on the last page of *Black Boy*. His story gives individual incarnation, too, to familiar by-products of this wrenching dislocation: in particular, the dysfunctioning of the family unit centered on the father and the growing family reliance on kin networks and female figures. A mother, an aunt, and a maternal grandmother supply Wright's family anchor when his father deserts them shortly after they reach Memphis, their first truly urban center.

But if it traces these familiar outlines, Wright's story can also remind us that the Great Migration was hardly a linear development for those who lived it and that every individual experience of this move had its own rich circumstantial history.

As *Black Boy* documents, Wright moved not once but many times on the road to Memphis and Chicago, these moves being driven by complex and shifting combinations of family disaster and family assistance, pursuits of opportunity and retreats from misfortune. Wright came to live in Jackson in 1918 because his grandparents had their home there, having moved from Natchez in 1916 to live near a son who bought them a house. Wright was thrown back on his grandparents' care by his mother's continuing disability following a stroke. In the three or four years before that, after the debacle brought on by her husband's desertion, Ella Wilson Wright had resettled herself and her young sons in various towns in Arkansas where she could find jobs, but had repeatedly moved back to her parents' house in Jackson when physical collapse, economic failure, or—in one case—racial violence forced her to. (Her career perfectly exemplifies the "frantic search for day work within the region" that Jacqueline Jones has found many black migrants to have undertaken "before heading for the Midwest or Northeast.") Like the Weltys, Wright, his mother, his grandparents, and the aunts and uncles who participated in the extended Wilson family move were among the new arrivals registered in Jackson's swelling population figures. Their conjunction will remind us that early-twentieth-century Jackson did not have one uniform history but grew through the confluence of several. Its development helped support many different social positions, a new world of economic marginality and urban poverty along with a new world of middle-class prosperity.

Though I have not seen them mentioned, these developments might be learned of from other sources than Wright and Welty. What *Black Boy* and *One Writer's Beginnings* tell us that we could scarcely know by other means is what it felt like to live in these social settings, what the world looked like when encountered from these points. Wright, we know, homogenized his experience to some extent in writing his autobiography, darkening and (so to speak) melodramatizing it in order to make himself the representative young black male in poverty, Black Boy. Manuscript drafts in Yale's Beinecke Rare Book

Library contain accounts of pleasure, considerate attention, and sheer non-crisis-ridden ordinary life that Wright later left out. But even with this more mixed evidence factored back in, Wright's early life is grim enough. Wright has given one of the most memorable accounts we have of what it is like to *live* poverty. His daily life is organized around gnawing hunger, the continual physical reminder of his lack of access to the first necessities of life. Emotional deprivations compound this physical lack. Wright is loved by his mother, someone too weak to help or protect him, a person who requires *his* sympathy and care. Otherwise his affective world is defined by family presences by turns incomprehensibly rejecting, irrationally repressive, sadistic, or simply indifferent.

The self that emerges from this world of deprivation is an antisocial loner. In *Black Boy*, Wright images himself as a kind of comprehensive juvenile delinquent, guilty by his own confession of arson, cruelty to pets, obscenity, graffiti writing, employee theft, and petty larceny. But above all Wright projects himself as the black youth as tensed-up aggressor, an armed assailant equipped now with a stick, as when his mother sends him shopping in Memphis's mean streets; now with a ring with sharp prongs, in the schoolyard of Greenwood, Mississippi; now with a knife, as in his fight with Aunt Addie; now with a razor, as in his fight with his Uncle Tom. No reader is likely to forget these sharply drawn images. But Wright's most powerful accomplishment in *Black Boy* is to teach us gradually to read this aggressiveness as a form of defensiveness, a defense against larger aggressions palpable to the black boy but invisible to us. In Wright's earliest chapters destructiveness seems to spring from within as a kind of overmastering, unaccountable daimonic urge, like Poe's imp of the perverse a *"mobile non motiviert,"* as when young Richard, on a whim, lights his grandmother's curtains on fire. Subsequent chapters begin to show what seem like impulsive self-assertions as proceeding from a desperate need to defend himself against forces that threaten to violate him from without. In the almost exclusively black-inhabited world of Wright's early chapters this would-be overpowerer is embodied in black characters, notably the family members who would beat the narrator and the schoolmates who would humiliate him. But as his social horizons expand, this terror-inducing force comes finally and most effectively to be embodied in distant whites: first the actual whites who, · motivated by racial and economic competition, murder his Uncle Hoskins (Wright writes of this episode of racial terrorism: "we . . . had fallen on our faces to avoid looking into that white-hot face of terror that we knew loomed somewhere above us"); then the increasingly disembodied whites projected through rumors of racial atrocities that circulate in the black community, psychic figures of white supremacy who make Wright feel the continual pressure of their "hate and threat" and who condemn him to be "continually reacting" to their impending hostility. A scene dear to me because it comes as close as we get to encountering Eudora Welty in the pages of *Black Boy* shows the workings of Wright's psychic life as a racially terrorized subject. When young Richard tries to raise money by selling his dog in a "white neighborhood [of] wide clean streets and big white houses," a pleasant young woman comes to one door, giving him a glimpse of the alien "cleanliness [and] quietness of the white world." But when this girl disappears into the house to look for her money, Wright cannot *not* attach this pleasant individual white person to the omnipresent, disembodied force of white terror that his world has instilled in him as the primary connotation of whiteness. In mounting anxiety he believes the girl must have gone to summon the force he expects and fears whites to bring to bear on blacks: a lynch mob.

Every social arrangement of early-twentieth-century Jackson, even the most seemingly innocent and progressive, enforced the inequality of the races. Jackson's up-to-date new public schools were of course closed to blacks, though a parallel, separate but never equal black school system imitated these developments with significant lags. The 1938 WPA Guide blandly reports that "gallery space is reserved for Negroes at the civic auditorium for all performances, but the number who attend is negligible": negligible perhaps because this facility

allowed blacks in on conditions that marked their difference
and inferior status. Wright's authority in *Black Boy* derives from
his unraveling, through an act of autobiographical introspec-
tion, of the intrapsychic drama that upheld this system of social
difference. In the world he remembers white supremacy need
hardly ever resort to actual violence because it has induced in its
black subordinates the felt menace of *possible* violence. Continually reacting against a threat of violation that is never visibly
caused, Wright's black boy remains trapped in a state of retalia-
tory, defensive aggression—a state that also condemns him,
since his provocation remains invisible, to appear to others as
an unmotivated criminal or "natural" delinquent.

Deprivation, exposure, dread, and entrapment are the psychic yields of Wright's early scene. By contrast, the operation of
Welty's way of life is to construct a thoroughly sheltered world.
Welty's mother and father sing in concert on the first page of
One Writer's Beginnings. From separate rooms, they work
together to create an atmosphere rich in concords. Through
their prosperity and, still more, through this conspicuous devotion to the creation of a happy home, Christian and Chestina
Welty as remembered in *One Writer's Beginnings* build a world
for Eudora that is rich with every advantage and shielded from
every distress. (Not every distress, obviously: the moving third
section of Welty's memoir suggests that through the very intensity of their love, Welty's parents made their inevitable death
the central trauma of their daughter's life.) Without minimizing
the rare qualities of Welty's mother and father as individuals, it
is useful to note the class dimension of this family project. In
the building of a carefully bounded world of family closeness, a
space of mutual involvement designed to shut out external
menaces (Welty calls it "a cocoon of our own"), Welty's family
exemplifies two of the deepest drives that identify the traditional middle-class family model: its inward-turning cultiva-
tion of domestic privacy and its high investment in the achievement of a sense of security.

Mentally grounded in this carefully created security, the
young Welty walks at her ease through her childhood's social

spaces, never fearing because never even *seeing* possible adversaries. The only violence remembered in *One Writer's Beginnings* is a violence of excessive parental protectiveness. In the unique appearance of a possible weapon in this book, Welty recalls her father taking a pocket knife and scoring the polished soles of her new shoes "all over, carefully, in a diamond pattern, to prevent me from sliding on a polished floor when I ran." (Actually, there is a second weapon: when the family drives north from Jackson to visit family in Ohio and West Virginia, there is "a loaded pistol in the pocket on the door of the car on Daddy's side," but since no use for this weapon is imagined, it produces only a momentary and slightly comic *frisson*.) If Wright cannot forget an omnipresent whiteness, Welty seems blithely oblivious to racial others. One black only, an old woman who sews for her mother and carries delicious gossip from house to house, appears in her remembered Jackson. As she strolls with perfect confidence through the world outside her home, Welty visits scene after scene of official segregation with no consciousness of their exclusionary or inferiorizing function. She is welcomed at a precocious age to the Jefferson Davis School with no awareness that public schools were a principal agency of racial discrimination. She amusingly recalls roller-skating through the rotunda of the state capitol at the head of her street, undisturbed by the knowledge that this seat of legal discrimination was not principally a playground. (In her account, Mississippi state legislators — Bilbo, too, one wonders? — appear in the role of comic lunkheads, losers in a spelling bee with her clever fourth-grade class.) A note from her mother wins Eudora entitlement to "read any book she wants from the shelves" of the Carnegie Library, "children or adult." "With the exception of *Elsie Dinsmore*," she adds with conscious comedy — but momentarily *un*conscious that this library was not open to black patrons with or without notes from home.

One Writer's Beginnings and *Black Boy* give a vividly exact picture of what terms like *privileged* and *underprivileged* would have meant in the context of an early-twentieth-century Southern city. We might even be tempted to propose that they show the two halves of the mental world created in the heyday of official segregation, that asymmetrical structure in which one party is condemned to feel itself perpetually in the intimidating shadow of the other while the other is freed *not* to think of *it,* to enjoy the pleasures of superiority without awareness of how they have been achieved.

But as soon as this suggestion is made we would at once need to add qualifications. One would be that these authors' childhoods do not represent "white" and "black" experience even for Jackson, Mississippi, circa 1920 but somewhat extreme points on a spectrum of such experience. Poorer whites than Welty would not have lived so screened from race and its attendant conflicts. Had Wright lived in the black middle-class world the WPA guide describes quite frankly—"not all the city's Negroes are unskilled laborers; many of the state's leading Negro lawyers, doctors and educators live here. . . . They own substantially built homes, make themselves a part of the city's economic life, and follow the sophisticated trends of the white population"—his outlook would have diverged less from Welty's. There is also reason to think that both Wright and Welty might have had a greater mixture of experience than their books record, concerned as they are to create a coherent impression. Wright, for instance, had a close and apparently confidential relationship with the Walls, a white family he worked for in his early teens. *Black Boy* leaves this out in order to make Wright's emerging racial consciousness be formed wholly in injury and rage.

But the greatest limitation of a polarized account of Welty as white privilege and Wright as black deprivation is that it gets the consequences of these origins exactly wrong. One use of *Black Boy* and *One Writer's Beginnings* should be to teach us to mistrust the absolute value of social privilege: for if one is a story all of advantage enjoyed and the other all of advantage withheld, the central paradox of these paired memoirs is that *both* are tales of writers' beginnings, of the laying of foundations for a literary career. Both of these remembered lives, not just the happy one, funded a writer's artistic consciousness. Both Welty's and Wright's youths wrote into them scenes and schemes of understanding that their work could later explore.

(Because virtually the whole of Wright's artistic capital lies in his knowledge of racism's psychic wounds, could we not say that Jackson funded Wright's career at least as generously as it did Welty's?) Whatever the content of their experience, Wright's and Welty's lives each also produced someone obsessed with the power of words and hungering to wield such power—produced, in short, someone determined to be a *writer*. Little as they recognized it, one result of their very different childhoods was to make them hold an ambition absolutely in common; but this is not to say that they held it on identical terms. A final thing their memoirs teach is that if both beginnings helped produce a will to write, those beginnings also put Wright and Welty in a different relation to writing: made this same activity mean, for them, profoundly different things.

I have noted that Welty's middle-class background is marked by her father's white-collar employment and her mother's leisure, by her family's inward-turning preoccupation with domestic life, and by her parents' energetic devotion to the care and rearing of their children. (Welty lists the organizing values of this class when she recounts her father's belief that "success in business was the solution to most of the problems of living—security of the family, their ongoing comfort and welfare, and especially the certainty of education for the children.") Here it can be noted that in its compulsive care for "the education of the children" Welty's family displays another profoundly middle-class habit. Her parents are both loving and constantly edifying, continually engaged in imparting to their children the mental skills that will make for success in life. Santa Claus brings these children "toys that instruct boys and girls . . . how to build things"—Tinker Toys, Erector sets, and other implements of pleasure and covert education. In their home the living room is so bookcase-lined that it is called "the library," and the dining room is a virtual reference room: "Here to help us grow up arguing around the diningroom table were the Unabridged Webster, the Columbia Encyclopedia, Compton's Pictured Encyclopedia, the Lincoln Library of Information, and later the Book of Knowledge."

Within this atmosphere of loving edification, family life and the experience of books become virtually indistinguishable to the growing Eudora. As a young child Welty is raised in a state where affection is expressed and intimacy effected through reading:

> I learned from the age of two or three that any room in our house, at any time of day, was there to read in, or to be read to. My mother read to me. She'd read to me in the big bedroom in the mornings, when we were in her rocker together. . . . She'd read to me in the diningroom on winter afternoons in front of the coal fire, with our cuckoo clock ending the story with "Cuckoo," and at night when I'd got in my own bed. Sometimes she read to me in the kitchen while she sat churning, and the churning sobbed along with *any* story.

As she grows up Welty's parents express their love for her through gifts of books: "I was presented, from as early as I can remember, with books of my own, which appeared on my birthday and Christmas morning. Indeed, my parents could not give me books enough." In doing so her parents are handing down their own experience of the book as sign of love. Chestina Welty, by her daughter's account a hedonistic reader who "sank into Dickens in the spirit in which she would have eloped with him," had her beloved collected Dickens as a gift from her father. Christian Welty's childhood *Sanford and Merton*, also still preserved in her family home, is a palpable symbol of his mother's love and loss:

> I had the feeling even in my heedless childhood that this was the only book my father as a little boy had had of his own. He had held onto it, and might have gone to sleep on its coverless face: he had lost his mother when he was seven. My father never made any mention to his own children of the book, but he had brought it along with him from Ohio to our house and shelved it in our bookcase.

These initiations do more than give Welty easy access to the world of reading and writing. They force on literacy certain experiential associations and so give it a determinate personal meaning. Welty comes to writing as to a parentally supported activity: "It was my mother who emotionally and imaginatively supported me in my wish to become a writer. It was my father who gave me the first dictionary of my own." In her childhood she comes to know writing as an emblem and instrument of family love: in Welty's home separated family members *write* each other every day. As she experiences it writing becomes an extension of a primary world of loving family security: "I think [my mother] was relieved when I chose to be a writer of stories, for she thought writing was safe."

Though he chooses not to emphasize them, Wright, too, was not without favoring forces in his coming into contact with writing, and it is unlikely that he would have become an author without their assistance. The most important biographical fact *Black Boy* conceals is that Wright's mother—like Welty's—had been a schoolteacher when she married, a status with no small meaning in a state with high black illiteracy rates. *Black Boy* reports in one short sentence that Ella Wright encouraged Wright's wish to read, but manuscript drafts suggest a warmer, fuller experience of education and togetherness: in one excised passage Wright remembers his mother helping him read accounts of the sinking of the Titanic. Later excisions make clear that Ella Wright, not after all so unlike the Weltys, cared for "education for the children" and made sacrifices on its behalf: during a brief stint of relative prosperity as a white doctor's assistant before her stroke, she enrolls Richard in a private school she can barely afford. By moving to Jackson, Richard also won access to something he would have lacked in another place: the most highly evolved public school system for blacks in the state. In 1921 he entered the Jim Hill School, like Welty's Davis School an elementary school recently built on his very street. He later attended eighth and ninth grade at Smith Robertson School, a black school not one quarter mile from Welty's home. (The cemetery one block from Welty's house was the boundary between black and white residential districts.) After this he could have continued in—and briefly began at—

Jackson's first black public high school, Lanier High, newly founded just when he reached this grade level.

But Wright is not wrong to report his world as characterized by relatively stark literary deprivation. These advantages, after all, were only comparative: they put him far ahead of the illiterate sharecropper's children he meets in the Delta while working for a black insurance agent, alter egos amazed by his urbanity and literacy, but they left him far behind many other contemporaries. With or without a teacher in the house, the family chaos of Wright's early life meant that he did not attend a full year of school until he was ten. A star pupil who caught up quickly, his slow start still meant that he finished ninth grade at Smith Robertson only in 1925, the year the same-aged Eudora Welty graduated from Central High. (Wright's speech as valedictorian, a major event in *Black Boy*, must have occurred within days of Welty's graduation.) Staffed as they must have been with devoted teachers, Wright's schools, in any case, were far from the equal of comparable white schools. Dalehite's history records persistent overcrowding and sharply inferior funding for Jackson's black public schools early in the century. Most black education was also heavily weighted against literature and liberal arts in Wright's youth, and in *Black Boy* he notes: "We never had any instruction in literary matters at school; the literature of the nation or the Negro had never been mentioned."

Welty's home world solicited her toward the printed word. Of her book-surrounded infancy she writes: "Still illiterate, I was ready for them, committed to all the reading I could give them." Wright had no such experience. In the stark poverty of his early years, books and reading materials were one more thing his family could not afford. When he moved to his grandmother's in Jackson this absence was reinforced by her religious fundamentalism, which was harshly antiliterary and made fiction especially—*lies*, by her reckoning—vigorously proscribed. According to *Black Boy*, it was not just in his home that literary writing was a foreign notion. When Wright writes his first story, the neighbor he finds to read it to has no idea what it is or why he would have wished to do it: "What's that for?" she asks of his story. Wright here images a kind of ultimate literary poverty, a world unfurnished with the means even to form the concept of writing as a valuable activity. "My environment contained nothing more alien than writing or the desire to express one's self in writing," he memorably concludes.

This state of affairs does not shut Wright out of the world of written expression. But it does mean that as he wins access to it, writing has other meanings constructed for it than the ones Welty learned. Wright's grandmother casts a pall of proscription over the "devil's work" of literary writing, but her boarder, a "colored schoolteacher," lets him into this taboo land. When Wright begs the teacher to tell him about the books she is always reading, she repeatedly refuses, but then whispers to him "the story of *Bluebeard and His Seven Wives.*" In this scene of initiation and arousal, interrupted by his grandmother just when they were "about to finish," imaginative writing comes to Wright as that which gives access to the real thing, the compelling and fulfilled world outside his life of harsh restriction: "The tale made the world around me be, throb, live. . . . I tasted what to me was life, and I would have more of it, somehow, someway."

Imaginative writing here projects poverty and racism's otherwise unavailable *other*, the other world of freedom and gratified desire his "real" life is bent on denying him. Hereafter throughout *Black Boy* writing accrues the specific meaning of resistance to spiritual impoverishment, a way out of deprivation and stuntedness. Unlike Welty, to whom the joys of writing are generously given, Wright must seize writing's pleasures and powers against the intentions of the institutions that preside over it. In a white supremacist magazine supplement that he unknowingly peddles, a print-culture instrument intended to enforce his inferiority, he gains access to Zane Grey stories and so finds a way imaginatively *out* of a restrictive reality: "a gateway to the world." In Memphis's Cossit Public Library, Wright too gains access to books, but by struggling *against* the library's policies of racial exclusion. Chestina Welty's letter of entitlement to the Carnegie Library—"Eudora is nine years old and has my permission to read any books she wants from the shelves, children or adult" — finds its weirdly inverted corollary in the note the eighteen-year-old Wright forges from a white patron whose illiterate servant he pretends to be: "Dear Madam: Will you please let this nigger boy have some books by H. L. Mencken?"

Seized against — not gratefully received from — the world that surrounds him, writing comes to Wright as a tool of resistance *to* that world, not of reattachment, comes indeed as aggression's better weapon found at last. In the Memphis library Wright famously discovers of Mencken: "Yes, this man was fighting, fighting with words. He was using words as a weapon, using them as one would use a club. Could words be weapons? Well, yes, for here they were. Then, maybe, perhaps, I could use them as weapons?" In what is plotted as the crisis of liberation in *Black Boy,* Wright discovers writing as substitute for razor or knife, a tool that can help him articulate the self-hood-damaging mechanisms of a racist society and so escape its cycles of entrapping aggression.

There is no such thing as Southern Writing if we mean something unified and homogeneous by that term, Welty and Wright teach us. The South, they show, has given birth to very different forms of writing — in other words, to writing produced on different understandings of what writing is and does — and it has done so because the different Souths that have overlapped in geographical space have given authors radically different acculturations, equipped them with different worlds of experience and so with different understandings of writing itself.

Wright's and Welty's careers have barely begun when their narratives end, and a full account of their literary acculturations would need to attend to further lessons learned in later scenes — including, for them as for all Southern writers, scenes outside the South. In Wright's case we would need to look at the organized sociabilities offered by the Federal Writers' Project and the John Reed Club, sites of the formation of his idea of authorship that reinforced the notion of literature as agent of resistance to social oppression. In Welty's case we would need to consider the literary initiations provided by a college education in the late 1920s; also the educations supplied by her early editors, first the New York group that included her eventual agent and supporter Diarmuid Russell, later the *Southern Review* editors who brought her to public prominence. (This group included Cleanth Brooks, father of the New Criticism and a major reinforcer, we can surmise, of her idea of writing as a medium of internally crafted meanings and universalized themes.) Welty's own work in the WPA would also bear important inquiry. Just as the Chicago WPA helped release Wright from the intellectual isolation of a Southern black, the WPA's Mississippi operations helped mitigate the insularities of Welty's white world. "[My job at the WPA] took me all over Mississippi, which is the most important thing to me, because I'd never seen it—except Jackson and Columbus—never," Welty said in an interview in 1977. "That experience, I think, was the real germ of my wanting to become a real writer, a true writer. It made me see, for the first time, what life was really like in this state. It was a revelation." (The WPA photographs collected in her volume *One Time, One Place* show what it was in particular—the black cultures of country and town—that Welty now came to see.) Suggestively, at the moment she embraced it as a vocation, Welty knew writing as the product of a protected childhood that helped her be aware of protectedness's costs and exclusions, at once an extension of and a way to probe the limits of her secure "cocoon."

But although these writers' literary acculturations are not over when their books conclude, the educations they record are not without consequences. The traces of their socially structured literary understandings are to be found in their mature works' different textures, tones, and projects, but even more in the stance they assume as they go about their work. As practicing authors Wright and Welty put forth virtually antithetical versions of the figure of the writer. Welty became the writer as homebody, moving back to her hometown before taking up her literary career, indeed moving back into her family's house in Jackson—the lifelong base of her literary operations. Wright

became the writer as exile, one whose career propelled him farther and farther from Mississippi — to Chicago, to New York,
finally to Paris. Two lines infinitely diverging but tracing paths
learned in the place where they had intersected: one that
defined writing as an extension of, one that made writing an
aggression against, a once-common home.

AT THE MILLENNIUM
AN AGENDA GOING FORWARD

At the turn of the millennium, the *Yale Daily News* asked me for my thoughts on the future. This piece identifies priorities as I saw them then. Many things called for here — need-blind admissions for international students, for instance — quickly came to pass. Many others were incorporated into the proposals of the 2003 Yale College Report. Reprinted from the *Yale Daily News*, January 12, 2000.

I HAVE ONLY ever made one prediction that came true. Having vowed that I would never thereafter speak on the subject, I addressed the history of millennial expectation in my freshman address to the class of 2000. In what some later called my "odometer speech," I cited the pathetic utterance of one participant in the American millennial excitement of the 1840s when the world didn't end on the appointed day — "still in the cold world" — and I predicted that our own millennial moment would be something similar: a thumping anticlimax.

Lo, it came to pass. The magic moment came and went with almost apocalyptic uneventfulness, and we too find ourselves not in a brave new world but rather in the same old one: the given world with all its familiar problems. But working to shape the real world was always going to be more interesting than waking up in the world beyond the need of effort. So if the students of Yale College find themselves still in the cold world, I say, Welcome back. Happy millennium. Let's get to work.

But however unreal it proved in other ways, the millennial moment makes a good time to think about the future. I have no confidence that we can see the far future in much detail. It's chastening to recall that, of the three greatest changes that took place here in the last hundred years – Yale's transformation into a world-class research institution, the introduction of the residential college system, and the opening of admission without bars of gender or social origin – not a single one was foreseen a hundred years ago. We should not delude ourselves that we could do much better at guessing how Yale will transform itself by the year 2100, but it would be wrong to have no dreams for the stretch of future that we can foresee. In this spirit, I offer a few ideas of goals we should work toward.

Each of Yale's great modern changes created new institutional structures as a way to realize a deep educational goal. The structures have become familiar realities, but we should not assume that their deep purposes have been perfectly or permanently secured. One key task for the future is to remember the ends to which current arrangements were devised and to press to ensure that the ends, not just the means, are achieved.

In the admissions revolution of the 1960s, Yale College clung to the notion that it was to be a training ground for leaders but revised its sense of what future leaders would look like. Embracing the notion that, in the coming world, society's most constructive contributors would come from every part of our culture, not a few privileged places, Yale opened itself to students of every origin who had the talent, creativity, self-discipline, and social generosity to get the good of this place. Having experienced the tail end of the old order, I can testify that we enjoy the benefit of this revolution every day. But we mistake if we think that the revolution has been accomplished once for all.

Need-blind admissions, the enabling condition for Yale's modern demographics, is hugely costly to the university, and in spite of the happy haze that this prosperous moment has induced, it would be possible to imagine a downturn that could threaten Yale's ability to uncouple merit and income. Yale has accrued a massive endowment for financial aid, but it would be wrong to let up now. Ensuring that Yale College remains open to talent regardless of family circumstance should remain the highest priority for this place.

Nor should we assume that, because each current class is far more diverse than was once the case, we have finished the work of opening. Having forced itself to think about who it was meant to serve, Yale in the last (the now-distant 20th!) century changed from one admissions profile to another. But there is some danger that, once such a change has been effected, we will grow accustomed to the new profile and let custom take the place of thought. In recent American history certain categories have been used to measure diversity, and past history gave ample reason for attention to these categories. But we should always worry that one moment's schema of inclusiveness may covertly exclude people not recognized in that schema. If openness to talent is a value, then it requires a persistent effort to look for talent, especially in places we might be unconsciously ignoring.

To mention one example, Yale (by some measures) "achieved diversity" with non-Canadian international students forming less than 2% of its population. This blindness has begun to be righted, but going forward Yale must increase its efforts to attract the most talented students from around the world—which means that we must also increase the aid they need to come here. But we should be on the lookout for other blind spots as well.

The residential college system has become such an integral part of Yale that it is almost impossible to believe that Yale existed without it for 230 years. Built to give handsome housing to students and their activities, since the advent of randomized assignment the colleges have come to serve a new function: to form a sense of community in a populace no longer unified by homogeneous social origins. The extent to which students actually realize the experience of learning to understand, respect, work with, and enjoy each other across multiple lines of difference remains, to my mind, the most amazing accomplishment of Yale's modern history.

But tolerance and community are always fragile achievements, and we must not assume that we are immune to the forces that menace them. Rebuilding the residential colleges will be one of the inspiring projects of future years. But as we restore the colleges, we must work just as hard to protect the spiritual reality of which they have become the physical sign: a community built on the most widely extended individual respect.

But every virtue is a defect seen from another point of view, and while I rejoice in the sense of community at Yale, I recognize that it comes at a certain price. There are schools whose internal culture has so little to offer that students naturally turn outward in search of interest and fulfillment. Yale's has so much to offer that students here naturally turn inward, with the result that the very richness of life here can breed an excessive comfort in the confines of the womb. To my mind, one of our priorities should be to thin the walls between college and the world: to make the exploration of life outside a greater part of Yale College education.

"Outside" should be understood to mean a hundred things, from New Haven's public schools to the global entrepreneurial system, and "education" should partly mean formal education — course work. We need to press to make sure our courses engage dimensions of reality, not just the internal logics of academic subfields. In right practice the distributional system would mean that no student would leave Yale without a strengthened grasp of the host of determinants — biological, psychological, cultural, environmental, linguistic, economic, political, and more — that shape each life.

But when I speak of a heightened emphasis on life outside the walls, I am not only thinking of academic applications. While I have no wish to convert Yale into a travel agency or vocational training camp, I do think Yale students would benefit from a far more aggressive introduction to what goes on in the world. The upgrades now under way at Undergraduate Career Services and the Office of International Education and Fellowship Programs will make major improvements in this area. But fully developed, these offices could do far more than advise on the technicalities of job hunting and formal study abroad.

They could be a real window on the world — or better yet, a lens: a device for calling blurry distant realities into sharp visual focus. Through these offices, Yale could help students win a detailed sense of opportunities that exist away from Yale and could spur them to go find what these opportunities might have to teach. Not that this work should be confined to these offices. As we fortify the formal curriculum, we should seize every occasion to bring people through the college who can supplement academic expertise with worldly wisdom in its hundred forms. Forging tighter links between current students and former ones who have made their way in the world — Yale alumni — would be one way to improve access to this broader knowledge.

I have room for one more agenda item, and from many other candidates I would choose this one. As it moves into the future Yale must keep strong in every phase of study, but if there is one that requires special attention, it is the sciences. Given the discoveries the sciences have made in our time and given their ever-growing role in the transformation of health care, environmental protection, the transmission of knowledge, and other central areas, science will form an increasingly important part of what an educated person needs to understand.

In face of this fact, to maintain its standing among the great centers of education, Yale cannot be content to have the sciences stay only as strong as they are now. We need to maintain and renew the areas where we are a national leader and add significant strength where we are not.

Academic science is hugely expensive, so when one says these things one is talking about huge investments in faculty and laboratory facilities. These investments are essential, and I am delighted that the University recognizes their necessity. But the person in my position would always want to plead that we make very sure, when we make these expenditures, that we actually get the educational benefits we had in mind from them.

There are universities that give virtually no thought to undergraduates in their scientific research activities, but Yale's genius has been to keep advanced research and undergraduate teaching in close relation, and that is the last thing we should give up now. By my lights, we will know that we have built science right at Yale when outstanding faculty have been equipped with state-of-the-art facilities; *and* undergraduate majors have even larger opportunities to participate in the work of discovery; and undergraduates with undecided interests begin migrating into this area through the fascination of its curriculum; and students who do not go on to a specialized mastery still emerge with a grasp of what science is good for, obtained not to check off a requirement but because the subject was too interesting to pass up.

"Still in the cold world"—well, it may be so. But the intractable-seeming given world is the one that every new world has been made out of, and when I look at Yale College I see challenge and opportunity on all sides. At this time we have the duty, but also the privilege, of making this place as great for the future as others made it in the past. We'll succeed in proportion as we keep in mind what, deep down, a university is for.

TAKING DEMOCRACY TO SCHOOL

In observation of the Yale tercentennial, Yale Law School Dean
Anthony Kronman organized a series of DeVane Lectures on aspects
of democratic theory and practice. Others spoke on democracy
and foreign policy, democracy and economics, and parallel topics.
My assignment was democracy and education. This gave a chance
to address issues in the air at that time on the national scene: the
No Child Left Behind initiative, the war on the SATs, affirmative
action, and the national obsession with selective college admissions.
First delivered on March 27, 2001.

IN OUR WORLD, the notion that the prospects for democracy
rest on the health of the education system has the status of a
self-evident truth. A person my age won't have known a time
when the fate of democracy was not felt to be riding on developments in the schools. The year I started fifth grade, I listened
every morning to radio news of the struggle to integrate the
public schools of Little Rock, Arkansas—news that made the
schoolhouse, the unremarkable scene of my own daily life,
appear as the site of the war against systematic inequality in
America. Later that year, when Russia launched the first space
satellite, Sputnik, I learned that the fate of world democracy
hinged on figuring out why Johnny can't read and Ivan can. In
more recent times, before it was overshadowed by concern for
homeland security, education had emerged as something like
the problem-in-chief in American political discourse. During
the presidential election of 2000, there was virtually no problem that failing schools were not alleged to have caused, as—
paradoxically, given that no one would say a good word for this
institution in its current form—there was virtually no ill for
which the reformed school was not proposed as the cure.

As these examples suggest, modern democracy tends to regard schooling not as a social process among others but as the very source of civic strength. So inevitable does the interdependence of democracy and education seem that two points might be worth making as correctives. The first is that this link is not a transcendental given. The ideas of democracy and the schooling needed to support it have no fixed shape: they have evolved over time, elaborated in changing ways by the larger action of social history. The other is that if this link has not been immutable, it has also not been straightforward or trouble-free. The demands that democracy has made on schooling have carried all the idealism, but also all the variegation and latent contradiction, that characterize that complex term, so that the history of democratic education has been the history of the puzzles of democracy quite as much as of its aspirations and successes. This essay looks at the history of democratic schooling partly to understand why that history should be problematic and partly to underline that those problems do indeed have a history—are in some cases far older and more enduring than modern consciousness might suppose.

It is well known that this nation's founders looked to Old World philosophers for their theory of representative government. It is not always remembered that those same philosophers also had ideas about education, which were imported together with their political thought. Locke, the author of the *First* and *Second Treatise on Civil Government*, was as familiar in America for his work *Of Education*, which urged the freeing of education from physical coercion. Noah Webster's 1787 essay "Of the Education of Youth in America" cited Montesquieu to the effect that while despotic governments would want to give little or no education to the people, a republican government would need for education to be widely available, since it would require "every class of people [to] know and love the laws." But if government by the people and schooling for the many were linked ideas, it would be a mistake to think that universal public education existed at the time of this nation's founding or that this idea figured in any prominent way in the early national agenda. In the late eighteenth century, most schooling was rudimentary and irregular, and education was by no means thought of as the monopoly of the schools. Family, church, and workplace were still the primary scenes of education in the early United States, with school serving as an occasional supplement.

One of the earliest elaborations of a democratic plan of schooling comes from Thomas Jefferson. Jefferson's draft legislation of a "Bill for the More General Diffusion of Knowledge" dates from the time just after the Continental Congress and the Declaration of Independence, when he returned to Virginia to undertake the revision or "revisal" of fundamental laws. Jefferson's revisals are an attempt to change the deep organizing structures of social life so as to generate a new social reality, the free, self-governing people of the Jeffersonian dream. His first proposed measure, the abolition of the laws of primogeniture and entail, aimed to break the means by which the passage of land and wealth perpetuated a hereditary ruling class. His second, a bill for establishing religious freedom, aimed to break the citizen's subordination at the level of inward conviction or belief. Jefferson's third revisal aimed to dismantle the mechanism by which those equipped with wealth and status won superior access to knowledge and the power knowledge brings: their privileged access to schools.

Jefferson's proposal envisioned a state-sponsored system that would make education available at three levels: the local elementary school, the regional grammar school, and the university. But the plan's most striking feature is not its integrated systematic organization, an idea unheard of in its time, but its fusion of this system with a sense of school's social mission. Jefferson's plan aims to create a political community in which the whole people, "every individual who composes their mass," will "participate of ultimate authority." Through their participation in the political process, citizens will be able to play the role of "guardians of their own liberty," watching for and warding off the degenerations Jefferson believes will result if power is allowed to pass from the people to their rulers. (Like all early republicans Jefferson's thinking is fraught with a sense of the fragility and vulnerability of the republican enterprise.) To equip citizens for the task of keeping their collective liberty safe, Jefferson writes, "their minds must be improved to a certain degree": in short, democratic government requires watchful citizens, and this requires a democratization of learning. It is noteworthy that Jefferson's scheme removes the Bible from elementary schooling and installs lessons in Greek, Roman, European, and American history in the first level of instruction. To Jefferson's mind, the one thing needful for future citizens is a working knowledge of political history, so they can spot the signs of government degeneracy or decay.

To fit Virginia's citizens for the work of citizenship, Jefferson proposes to establish a local school every five or six miles, where all children will be guaranteed three years' schooling at local taxpayers' expense. To equip especially capable pupils for future careers as public leaders, he plans a selection mechanism to give the most gifted access to further schooling "without regard to wealth, birth, or other accidental condition or circumstance." In order to "avail the state of those talents which nature has sown as liberally among the poor as the rich," at the end of three years of universal public education Jefferson would "chuse the boy, of best genius" in each school "of those whose parents are too poor to give them further education" and send him at public expense to one of twenty grammar schools to be founded throughout the state. After a year or two of trial at this level, "the best genius" at the new school would be chosen to receive a free six-year course of grammar school education. At this point, half the students would be qualified to be teachers and their education would be discontinued, and the half "of still superior parts" would be sent on to the College of William and Mary.

This blueprint is a brilliant work of civic imagination, but Jefferson puts deep paradoxes of democratic education on display in the act of unfolding a democratic educational vision. We could start with the fact that Jefferson's scheme was not adopted. It failed partly because Virginia voters were unwilling to entrust their local schools to a statewide system, an unimaginably remote and unreal entity at this time, but largely because they refused to assume the tax burden the scheme would entail. This would not be the last time that financial considerations would trump civic ambitions in the history of American schooling: this episode reveals that that tension between dreams and costs is endemic to democratic education, having been present since the creation. But what is most interesting about the fate of Jefferson's plan is not that it shows public high-mindedness at war with public tight-fistedness but that it reveals contradictions within the concept of "the democratic" itself. Jefferson's scheme was democratic in one sense of the word. It created equal access to school without regard to family income or status. Its defeat was democratic in another sense of the word. It resulted from the action of majority rule, government by the consent of the governed. This early chapter teaches that "democracy" encompasses not one but many different values, including—as here—directly competing ones; and that education can bear the weight of these plural goals only at the cost of making school the place where conflicts among democratic values are fought out.

A second paradox of Jefferson's scheme is even more flagrant to modern eyes. Jefferson would make school the great equalizer, *the* tool for neutralizing differences of income and family standing, but there are striking limits to the equality it creates. Slaves are not included in the people the school serves, and we can further note that the unspecified children who go to grade school silently metamorphose into the "boy" who might be chosen to go on. These are the habitual discriminations of an older world, but Jeffersonian selectivity does not stop there. His whole three-tier apparatus is an elaborate sorting device, a mechanism for separating out the person of superior parts and blessing him with further advancement. When Jefferson speaks of best geniuses being "raked from the rubbish," the limits of his egalitarianism come clear.

Jefferson's vision displays one of the most vexing contradictions that has attached to democratic education, the way an educational system designed to negate received social hierarchies can end up generating new inequalities of its own. This problem again derives from the tension between democratic values — here, democracy as the equalization of social lots and democracy as the creation of individual opportunities. In this case, the conflict is intensified by the fact that school reinforces democracy's egalitarian *and* anti-egalitarian or individualistic programs through its very structure. On the one hand, school as Jefferson conceives it equalizes opportunity. If there are enough schools and the public will pay the teacher, then everyone can learn literacy and civics. On the other hand, the essential nature of school in Jefferson's idea is that it plots a progression from lower to higher learning and measures and rewards differences of achievement as students struggle up this ladder. As long as school has the function of discriminating superior from inferior performance and aiming those with different school records toward different social fates — an idea deeply rooted in the idea of school to this day — then formal education can be only an ambiguous ally to the democratic project: an instrument for neutralizing inequalities of station and wealth in some measure but the potential creator of new differences in their place, differences based this time on educational performance itself.

Nothing remotely resembling Jefferson's plan came into being during his lifetime. By the end of the 18th century some states had made preliminary moves toward establishing universal education — in 1795 Connecticut voted to sell off the state's land claim in Ohio (the so-called Western Reserve) and invest the proceeds for the support of public education. But 60 years after Jefferson wrote his revisal, American schools were still haphazard and chaotic, as measured by the fact that toddlers were sometimes dumped into the same schoolroom as older children and teachers taught reading from whatever different books their pupils' families happened to own. The great push for systematized public education came from the generation of school reformers active in the North and Midwest in the 1830s and 1840s, the so-called Common School Movement. This group envisioned and won public and legislative support for "school" as Americans have known it since: something open to all children, paid for by public taxes, running for set terms, with pupils divided into progressive grades, taught by professionally certified instructors, under local control, but governed by state norms overseen by a state board of education.

It is important to remember that what the Common School Movement envisioned was only gradually enacted. Though its plans were fully articulated by 1840, it was decades before what it promoted came to full reality even in states where progress was most advanced. But if this movement eventually succeeded, as it did, it was because it fused a detailed plan for a school system with a persuasive theory of this plan's social value. Horace Mann was not the only effective advocate of this cause but he was its most skilled rhetorician. A crucial part of Horace Mann's work as Secretary of the Massachusetts State Board of Education was to fashion a rationale for the new common school and render it publicly compelling. The Annual Reports that Mann wrote between 1837 and 1848, one of the great contributions to the literature of democratic education, elaborate a far richer role for schooling in democratic culture than what Jefferson had proposed sixty years before.

In these Reports, Mann repeats, but marks as trite, the thought that people need education in order to play their political role in a republic. This is already a truism by Mann's time, and he hastens to supplement it with new rationales. This argument is joined on one side by a theory that school's real work is the psychological formation of the young, and that the service the school can render the republic is less to teach civics lessons than to instill the inward dispositions of republican civic character — especially the habit of self-government, which equips children (in the Ninth Annual Report's words) to be "a constituent part of a self-governing people."

Elsewhere, Mann devises an economic argument for the need for schooling in American democracy. In the Annual Report of 1848 Mann looks across the ocean to an England convulsed by the strife brought on by industrial and capitalist development, the Britain of the Chartist Movement and Engels's *The Condition of the Working Class in England*. Reflecting that Massachusetts is the lead site for these developments in America, Mann asks: what can prevent our being visited by the same destructive disparities of wealth and power? The answer (as always for Mann!) is common school education. If education is universally available, then Americans need not be mere wage slaves at the mercy of the owners of great capital. They will be skillful; inventive; productive contributors to the process of development. Fueled by this mass brainpower, American society will not collapse into class war over a static pot of wealth. The spread of knowledge will create an ever-expanding economy, and so an ever-expanding world of opportunity in which all can win advantage. "Knowledge and abundance sustain to each other the relation of cause and effect," Mann writes in a memorable passage. "Intelligence is a primary ingredient in the Wealth of Nations."

Mann here develops the notion that democratic citizenship requires not just participation in the political process but also participation in a growing economy, an economy fueled by the intellectual capital its members share. Elsewhere he finds an argument in the heterogeneity of the American population, which permits him to propose yet another role for schools in a democracy: as the creator of a common culture for a people of mixed origins. Mann's First Report contains a surprisingly early reflection on the problem of private schools. The parents in any elementary school, Mann reflects, will likely contain two elements: the apathetic, those who care too little about what's going on in their kids' school, and the heavily invested, those who care if anything too much. (Who was it who said that the only new history is the history we have forgotten?) Rather than subject their children to the low average of the whole group's expectations, he reasons, these parents will want to pull their children out of the common school to give them superior advantages elsewhere. But when they send their kids to private school, parents will also shift their interest to the new place ("the heart goes with the treasure"), leaving the public school further impoverished by the withdrawal of their commitment and concern. The whole voucher debate is here in embryo.

Writing at the very birth of mass immigration as a feature of American life, Mann is already foreseeing how school could become the site for the sorts of social separations our later history has made all too familiar. But as usual with Mann, if school is part of the problem, it is the whole of the solution. Because of the tendency to social segregation in American life, Mann writes, it is more important than ever that elementary schools draw in the whole population. The goal of the common school is to be the thing people have in common, to *create* the experience of living together and knowing each other that may be lacking in the so-called "community" outside its walls. "It is on this common platform, that a general acquaintanceship should be formed between the children of the same neighborhood. It is here, that the affinities of a common nature should unite them together so as to give . . . a stable possession to fraternal feelings, against the alienating competitions of subsequent life."

One thing I have learned from the study of Horace Mann is that as the public school system has been elaborated over the course of American history, school has been asked to take on more and more problems and become the solution to more and more social ills. It might occur to us that one reason schools succeed imperfectly in teaching things like reading or math is that such instruction is the least of what modern democracy asks them to accomplish. Mann was the great seeker-out of problems the school could volunteer to shoulder, and the mark of his and his colleagues' success is that, for all its limits, the school they designed continues to be a key symbol of democratic hope. When I edited the journals of Charles W. Chesnutt, the chief African-American writer of the post–Civil War generation, I learned that the first thing the freed blacks of Fayetteville, North Carolina, did when the Civil War ended was to buy a plot of land with their own funds to build a public grade school on the New England model. (By means of this investment, black children in Fayetteville had public grade schools before their white contemporaries.) Their choice says what this school had come to symbolize: the way to knowledge, freedom, and full civic enfranchisement.

But like Jefferson's, this ideal carries tensions within it, two of which might be quickly mentioned. Seen one way, the school of the Common School Movement is the dream agent of democracy, creator at once of individual enablement and social community. But looked at in another light, it would appear to foster a very different social reality: systemwide regulation, the reign of standardized ordering devices—the school day, grades, teacher certification, the state board—the whole panoply of modern bureaucracy. Though they can be separated in theory, in actual history the democratization of schooling and the bureaucratization of schooling formed parts of a single process in America. We know the consequence: we sometimes get the democratic yields schooling promises, but we always get the bureaucratic ones, and the more inspiringly democratic a reform is made to sound, the more we can fear that that its leavings will be bureaucratic. In the most recent national debate, who would not favor tests and mandated standards if they keep schools from passing off an inferior education in socially disadvantaged areas? This has been tolerated far too long, and there is obvious sense to the thought that the way to address unequal social fates in later life is to provide more equal educational enablement in early life: to leave no child behind. But given that only the bureaucratic part of this program—the newly mandated tests—will be enforceable, it will require special effort to be sure that we get the reality of new enablement, and not just a new mass of official exercises and quantifying instruments.

On another front, Mann's school promises the creation of a common culture, but it is easy to suspect that this culture may be more common to some than to others. It is fascinating to watch Mann maneuvering against all the foes lined up against the common school and threatening to fracture his community of the whole: the private school with its limited class audience; the parochial school with its limited religious audience; the partisan school with its limited political audience, and so on. Over against these foes Mann labors to imagine things we could all be taught together, lest we be condemned to live in separate camps and at the mercy of the strongest faction. Since it is easy to underestimate the challenge he is facing, I find this part of Mann's work intelligent and even moving, but for all that, the "we" he proposes fits some groups very differently from others. His culture of self-government will fit us fairly comfortably if "we" have grown up in the antebellum American North, with its heavy promotion of internalized self-discipline, but if we have just "made a voyage across the Atlantic," as a hundred thousand Irish did in the year this line was written, we will have been "dwarfed under the despotisms of the Old World" and will need to have our deep character structures made over. (More work for the common school!) So too the nondenominational religious teaching he favors may seem of universal value to us if we are Christian and more particularly Protestant but will read like coercive proselytizing if we are from another faith.

We can fault Mann for the limits of his toleration, and we could all name schools that have favored children of some origins and marked others as inferiors to be made over. But the problem here is not a function of some person's or some institution's failings: it derives in part from a problem with the idea of democratic education itself. That idea is extraordinarily inspiring, but the moral glow it casts tends to conceal the fact that this term contains different and even opposite meanings, all of which have their legitimacy but not all of which tend to be held in mind at once. Mann gives prominence to the idea that democratic education needs to create an ethos that provides for collective agreement about collective rights. If we doubt that this is important, we should reflect that where such agreement is lacking, individuals and groups are wide open to violation by those who despise them. On the other hand, when we criticize Mann's enforced monoculturalism we are giving priority to an equally central democratic value: the right of the minority not to be victimized by the majority and the right of individuals not to have their beliefs constrained by the state. The harder Mann pushes for a culture of the whole, the more he calls up the critique of the whole's coercions of other cultures. Historically, the movements to protect children from victimization by schooling conducted in English or in an alien faith were contemporaneous with the Common School Movement and products of its success, and modern arguments for bilingual education and against secular humanism can be found virtually fully formed in the mid-19th century. (Catholics of that time resisted the enforced culture of the public schools long before Protestant fundamentalists did, and the people pushing for public education in their own tongue were not Hispanics but Germans and Norwegians.) Here and not only here, a common problem of democratic education is that those who embrace it can become so enthusiastic about one of its values as to be oblivious to the fact that they are negating another. The solution can't lie in simplifying the problem, whose complexity is the essence of its reality. It can only lie in being aware of the plurality of goods to be served and mediating thoughtfully among them.

Over the last century, primary school has continued to supply the main arena for staging democratic education's new ambitions and fighting out their attendant conflicts, but in the 20th century it has been joined by other venues. The most salient development of American education in the last hundred years has been the increased schooling of the population—by which I mean both the incorporation of the whole school-age population into school and the extension of time normally spent in school. The historian David Tyack estimates that the average American had only five years' formal education in the year 1900. By 1940, however, a number approaching 50% of American children had been to high school, the novel invention of the post–Civil War years. And since World War II, in a development that would have been unthinkable a hundred or even 60 years ago, the notion of adequate education has expanded for a larger and larger sector of the population to include the idea of college. Higher education has been the great growth sector in the postwar educational economy. Something like 2 million Americans went to college in 1951, but the number had grown to 4 million by 1961, and the *Chronicle of Higher Education* reckons that that number stood at more than 15 million by the year 2001 — with 11.8 million in public and 3.4 million in private colleges and universities, 9.3 million in four-year and 5.8 million in two-year institutions.

In the context of this essay, the meaning of this growth will, I trust, be clear. In our lifetime, higher education, for centuries an arcane domain for the few, has been annexed to the expanding empire of mass educational opportunity. And as college has become the great new site of democratic opportunity, it has also become a new object of public fixation and vexation, the new place for democratic controversies to be fought out.

I can only gesture at the factors that have driven the expansion of higher education. The first are those changes in the modern economy that continue ever more sharply to stratify employment opportunities and the educational attainment they require. This underanalyzed development has worked to revalue high school education, a relative rarity and a badge of advanced training a century ago, into a minimal preparation for most jobs and an insufficient qualification for a good one. This change has created a need and an ambition for higher-education where none had previously existed; and other developments have allowed this need to be much more widely met. I have in mind the rapid growth of the higher-education system, which created millions more places for possible students, and the not-unrelated growth of the economy itself, which created billions more dollars to pay for this new necessity.

In modern times, the conjunction of these new social facts has created two quite different consequences: first, massive new enrollment in many parts of the higher-education system, and second, massive new competition for places at certain schools. At selective institutions, increased external demand has meshed with an internal development that was by no means inevitably linked to it (Nicholas Lemann's *The Big Test* is the best chronicle of this development): conversion to an admissions system that gave much more weight to scholastic aptitude and academic performance. To oversimplify a little, in America's leading private universities, gentlemanly accomplishment had long been the main qualification for admission, with intellectual ability and attainment welcomed in appropriate measure but not by any means the dominant criterion. In the 1930s, in the middle of the Great Depression, Harvard President James Bryant Conant instituted an increased emphasis on intellectual aptitude in admissions, but as usual the change worked its way through the system fairly slowly. At first, Lemann shows, Harvard used its new meritocratic academic criteria to judge the admission only of scholarship students. It took three decades for the new admissions calculus to thoroughly succeed in delegitimating and replacing the older standards at Harvard and schools of its sort.

The more academically oriented admissions system was devised in quite a different world from the one in which it triumphed — really, it is a late creation of the Progressive Era. Once embraced, it served an increasingly important intrauniversity function: as universities began their evolution into the scenes of specialized knowledge creation they are today, this admissions policy supplied a new, more intellectual breed of student for a new, more professionalized breed of professor. But though it was devised for other occasions, in the late 1950s and 1960s this new admissions system came under the pressure of a new social development. Admissions policy at selective schools was not the Civil Rights movement's principal target, but in the changed world the Civil Rights movement created, selective universities became inevitably more conscious of and more embarrassed by everything that seemed to make them agents of discriminatory privilege. The fortuitous conjunction of these developments produced the great admissions revolution that we are on the far side of. I speak as one who lived through this change. In 1964 I entered a Yale College that was consciously increasing its outreach to public high schools but that was still — and still congratulated itself on being — all male. In 1968 I graduated from a Yale College that had made a decisive shift away from recruitment at feeder schools and that was on the verge of announcing that it would admit women. In 1972 I started teaching at a Yale College where the students were men and women from many different backgrounds and where students showed far more interest in their studies than had been the norm so short a while before – not surprisingly, since the democratization of admissions and the academicization of admissions criteria formed part of a single process.

But I have been arguing that democratization brings expanded controversy together with expanded opportunity, and so it has proved in this case. As *The Big Test* establishes in fascinating detail, when President Conant became interested in the Jeffersonian project of opening education to merit irrespective of family circumstance, as the means to calibrate merit he chose an intelligence test that measured scholastic aptitude – the dreaded SAT. As it has grown to its current massive use, the SAT has been essential to the opening of opportunity, giving the mentally adept a way to demonstrate their prowess and win advancement independent of family status. But when an instrument was adopted that seemed to yield a standardized, nationwide measure of objective merit, that same instrument could then create other, unforeseen consequences, ones we know well.

The SAT registered differences of performance between white and African-American students at all income levels, thus creating a quandary. If test disparities were allowed to stand uncorrected, then this measure could supply a new basis for group discrimination, a new means to enforce exclusions from high-level social opportunity. Given this country's painful racial history and the role schools have played in the enforcement of American racial inequality, these outcomes were unacceptable to large sections of the public and virtually all universities. Like other sites of opportunity, school systems devised ways to mitigate the pure rule of test scores so as produce a result more adequately inclusive of the social whole – a democratic (i.e., equalizing, inclusionistic) corrective to the antidemocratic action of a democratic (i.e., meritocratic, individual-opportunity-creating) instrument.

But once this move was made, the test could cut the opposite way. As Lemann notes, when there was no uniform measure of merit, there were no grounds to document one person's unfair treatment for someone else's advantage. But a scheme that required objective tests but then corrected the results with affirmative action protocols created a rich new ground for grievance and resentment. The Supreme Court's *Baake* decision gave tenuous legitimacy to a policy of mediation among the different democratic imperatives that came into collision over affirmative action, but 20 years later, that mediation has produced no secure consensus. This issue is still the subject of constant court battles, and we seem to have arrived at a new historical turn in which the SAT itself, unwitting "cause" of so much contention, seems about to become the agreed-on victim for all sides' collective wrath. In the winter of 2001 Richard C. Atkinson, the President of the University of California system, called for the abolition of the mandatory SAT I in admissions consideration, and Lemann makes a similar case in the conclusion to *The Big Test*.

When I hear proposals of this sort, I feel powerful sympathy with the frustration that fuels them, but I can't help suspecting that frustration is generating the fantasy of a simple solution: Kill the evil test and the good democratic world will return! The charges against the SAT are now well known. Every newspaper reader or TV watcher knows that, taken in large aggregates, student scores on this test rise with parental income, and that the better off can afford prep courses that artificially enhance their children's appearance of brilliance. Further, as President Atkinson has emphasized, this test can corrupt schooling by leading teachers to teach too exclusively toward this one fateful event. (Atkinson claims that California eighth graders now spend school time drilling thought patterns like "untruthful is to mendaciousness as circumspect is to caution": the source, no doubt, of the complex vocabularies for which Valley girls and boys are famous.)

These are weighty arguments, but a fair-minded person would want to post some items on the other side of the ledger. Given the perplexities of this moment, it is easy to forget that American higher education has in fact opened itself to talented individuals from a large variety of previously disparaged backgrounds in the last 40 years, and that devices like objective test scores have played no small part—continue to play no small part—in establishing their claims to admission. These results are now taken for granted, but they would not be assured if the instrument that enabled them were to be discarded. In my view, it would be well to be frank about who is going to lose in the next change of standards as well as who will gain. It would be well to foresee, in other words, what new problem of democratic education this fix of the current one would cause.

In any case, unless selectivity itself (the real culprit) can be made to go away from college admissions, there will always be competition, and thus the need for some ground for choosing among well-qualified contenders. When the SAT is repudiated, what will take its place, and what will guarantee the superior fairness of its discriminations? Lemann proposes replacing the scholastic aptitude test with an achievement test that would measure mastery of things actually studied in the high school curriculum. That sounds reasonable; but if the current test offers a very partial index to intelligence, in what way will this new one be a fuller gauge, and how will it fend off covert social advantage? Won't students from strong school systems outperform those from weaker ones on such tests—and if they do, how much advantage should we tolerate before we take steps to correct it? Lemann is particularly upset by the fact that high-achiever parents are now desperate to pass on the advantage of superior education to their not quite so formidable children. (Horace Mann saw it coming). But if overinvested parents have corrupted the old selection scheme, why would we assume they would give up in face of the new one, rather than hire even better tutors for the new big test?

On the other hand, if we replace a single test as a measure of an applicant's qualifications with (in the word of the hour) "holistic assessment," how are we to expect the public mad at "objective" standards to tolerate the subjectivity the new evaluation would require? And when one's child's whole personhood has been assessed and found wanting instead of just his or her scholastic aptitude, can we really expect the decisions to win a greater degree of public acceptance? Though current debate often overlooks the fact, selective private universities have always used a much broader form of evaluation in which the SAT scores are weighed as one item among many—without winning notably greater happiness with their negative decisions.

I am not speaking in defense of the SAT. After all these years its limits and usefulness are both well known. But I am speaking against the notion that the SAT is in any simple sense the heart of our problem. Our problem is not a flaw in the measuring tool and is not to be solved by rejiggering the instrument. It derives from the difficulty of deep questions about how merit itself should be defined for the purpose of university admissions and how this opportunity should be fairly distributed. These are not questions on which our society can be expected to come to easy agreement, but there will be no reaching even the most fragile solution except by engaging the real questions and exploring them in a searching way. In this struggle (should we be so lucky to have it), the helpful position will be one that acknowledges the authentic difficulty of the issues and recognizes the partial legitimacy of many competing answers.

To give a taste of the problem of judgment in this domain, I could say a word about the admissions philosophy of the school I know, which will find echoes at other selective colleges. Yale College looks for students with quick, inquiring minds. Such intelligence is the prerequisite for admission not because it is the only human value but because it has special relevance to the nature of such a school. Having amassed the resources of learning and inquiry, the university has a legitimate interest in sharing them with the students who will make the fullest use of these resources and contribute most vigorously to the unfolding of understanding. (This means that universities have legitimate interests that are not democratic interests.) But since the active, thoughtful play of mind is what this place requires, we do not measure intellectual potential mechanically. We look not just for dutiful accomplishment but for deeper traits of curiosity and mental independence, and we consult every available form of evidence—aptitude and achievement scores, grades, recommendations, the candidate's own writing—to help gauge this elusive potential. At the same time, a school that sees its mission as training students who will make constructive contributions to the world will look for many traits of character beside academic intelligence narrowly defined: traits like drive, commitment, the sense that gifts carry an obligation to use them well, a sense of the importance of living in and for a larger community.

Now, is this way of proceeding democratic? No, in that it rewards differences of gift and accomplishment; but yes, in that it opens doors for individual talent without regard to family background or ability to pay. No, in that we hope our students will distinguish themselves in later life; but yes, in that we hope that distinction will lie in their service to the social whole. No, in that we do not aim to "represent" the public through a fixed demographics in our student body. But yes, in that we actively seek talent from every sector of society and recognize that measuring differences of personal promise will require some reckoning of differences in advantages enjoyed. Adjudicating among competing values before the particulars of individual cases is the hard work of admissions. It is of the nature of things that neither the individual decisions nor the principles on which they are made can be beyond dispute.

When I call the attack on the SAT a false diagnosis of the college admissions problem, I mean that the real difficulty lies in agreeing on *what* is to be measured and *why*, not how. But I would also suggest that this attack may take attention away from other sides of the problem that are no less serious. First and most obviously, there is no point worrying about inclusiveness at the point of college admissions if we do not first make sure that many more people have a chance to be contenders for such admission. The scope of possible democracy in colleges will always be predetermined by the availability of excellent training before college, and this will require not just mastery of fundamentals—crucial though that is—but access to everything that provokes and expands the mind. Second, while controversies about tests and test scores have grabbed the headlines in recent years, there is reason to think that the real thing we should be worrying about is the money.

As Jefferson already recognized, the creation of educational opportunity requires someone to foot the bill. The past decades have witnessed two historically unprecedented developments in this area, the expansion of mass educational opportunity at relatively low cost at public colleges and universities and the adoption of need-blind admissions and need-based aid at the most selective private schools. But there is some danger that both of these may be coming under threat. Without much national attention, many states have moved to give students with good high school averages a free ride at a state college in hopes of keeping top students in the state. In practice this has rewarded students whose families could have paid the tuition while reducing admissions opportunities for the financially disadvantaged. But if "to those who have, much is given" becomes the implicit aid policy of public education, we could witness a restriction of opportunity at the financial end even as it is being nominally expanded at the level of official criteria. On the other side, recent financial aid improvements at a handful of wealthy private universities will increase the pressure on schools with smaller endowments to consider a return to merit-based aid if their competitive position erodes. But if need-blind admission and need-based aid should go by the board at a significant number of schools, then even more aid money will be chasing the well-to-do — a threat to democratic opportunity far graver than the choice of tests.

I have been focusing on college admissions, but my point applies to a far wider range of issues. I might state it this way. We do not do sufficient justice to the fact that the alignment of the words "democratic" and "education" is a fairly recent historical development. For centuries education had no democratic component or aspiration: the thought that schooling too should be of the people and for the people is a glorious invention of relatively recent times. But to say that it is glorious is not to say that it is unproblematic. Democracy in schooling means many things, not all of them achieveable in full measure at the same time; and when schools inspire frustration, it is often not because they have failed of their democratic mission but because they have achieved some part of this mission at the expense of another.

Solving these conundrums — working through the difficulties in a thoughtful and constructive way — will be the ongoing task of every community that cares about democratic education. In this process, two things will always be of the essence: keeping alive a full, generous, expansive dream of what education itself could be; and taking pains to entrust the work of teaching to the most devoted and inspiring of our contemporaries, those best geniuses who can make education happen. There's plenty of work ahead.

Works Cited

Thomas Jefferson, "A Bill for the More General Diffusion of Knowledge" and *Notes on the State of Virginia*, Query XIV, reprinted in *Writings* (Library of America, 1984).

Carl F. Kaestle, *Pillars of the Republic: Common Schools and American Society* (Hill and Wang, 1983).

Nicholas Lemann, *The Big Test: The Secret History of the American Meritocracy* (Farrar, Straus and Giroux, 1999).

Horace Mann, Annual Reports to the Massachusetts Board of Education, 1837–1848, selections reprinted in *The Republic and the Schools: Horace Mann and the Education of Free Men*, ed. Lawrence Cremin (Columbia University Teachers College, 1957).

Noah Webster, "On the Education of Youth in America," in *Essays on Education in the Early Republic*, ed. Frederick Randolph (Harvard University Press, 1965).

FREE SPEECH AND ITS
DISCONTENTS

As Dean it was my responsibility to enforce the widest respect for the right to free expression, a value all subscribe to until their own beliefs are seriously crossed. My in-the-trenches experience with this issue gave me a profound continuing education. It taught me, among other things, the value that conflicts over freedom of expression can have as an agent of education. Delivered to the Association of Yale Alumni, April 26, 2002.

I HAVE BEEN ASKED to address the subject of free speech in the university. I begin with a fact you may not know. Yale was founded 300 years ago, but it was emphatically not founded on the principle of free speech or free inquiry. Yale's creators founded a second New England college in no small part to cure the freethinking they felt had descended on Harvard. Their intention was to create a place where an undeviating Protestant Congregationalist orthodoxy could be passed intact from teacher to student until the end of time. In Yale's founding document, the charter of what was first called the Collegiate School of Connecticut, they spoke of the goal of "Perpetuating the Christian Protestant religion, by a succession of Learned and Orthodox men" – with "learned" and "orthodox" used as virtually synonymous terms.

So little did these founders associate the university with free expression that in Yale's 18th-century regulations, one detects a wish virtually to outlaw speech itself, at least on the part of students. The regulations of 1741 state that "all students should be slow to speak and avoid . . . profane swearing, lying, needless asseverations, foolish garrulings, chidings, strifes, railing, gesting, uncomely noise, spreading ill rumor, divulging secrets and all manner of troublesome and offensive behavior."

I recount this bit of history to underscore that the link between universities and free speech is not an immutable given. So far from being natural or eternal, this link has been forged together with the development of the modern university, and, as its context, of a certain sort of modern society.

When Yale was founded, it's worth remembering, there was no Bill of Rights or First Amendment, no constitutional rule that Congress could make no law that would abridge the freedom of speech, and no civil society in which free speech could be claimed as a right. That right was established in this country in 1789, almost a century after Yale was created, and codified an Enlightenment understanding that was then a relatively new idea. The notion that free speech had a special place in universities and that the university had a special mission to guard it arose later yet, together with a new idea of the university itself. This idea was first brought to birth in Germany in the early 19th century through the labors of Wilhelm von Humboldt and those who worked with him to found the new university at Berlin. This is where the distinctive features of what we know as the research university were first laid down. Its novelty lay not just in a new system of faculty positions or a new logic of specialization but in the new understanding of truth and the university's relation to it.

Yale's original or founding concept, we could say, was that there is such a thing as the truth; that virtuous and learned people know it; and that the function of the university is to pass on that truth in an unchanging form. Humboldt's different concept can be heard in his statement: "Everything depends on holding to the principle of considering knowledge as something not yet found, never completely to be discovered, and searching for it relentlessly as such." The university began to be remade as a research university the day it embraced the notion that truth is something brought into being through the labor of human understanding—something we never arrive at as at a final point or finished possession but are always striving and groping toward. Within this concept, the mission of the university is not to pass on an unchanged truth through a succession of the

learned but to host the endless labor, carried on from generation to generation, needed to come closer to the truth: the work
of challenging the adequacy of what currently passes for the
truth, attempting to seize it more fully, and making that understanding available to others so they can move beyond it to a yet
fuller realization.

It was under the aegis of this concept that the new-style
German university put in circulation two ideas that we are intimately familiar with, even if we have forgotten their origin. One,
what von Humboldt called *Lehrfreiheit*, is the freedom of teachers in their teaching, the idea that faculty must be allowed the
free exercise of their powers of inquiry. The other, *Lernfreiheit*, is
the freedom of students in their learning. Strikingly, these new
freedoms were not conceptualized as legal rights or requirements, though they arose not long after the First Amendment.
Instead, they were proposed as requirements of the university's
foundational object, knowledge. They are the freedoms teachers
and students need to be agents of inquiry, partners in that endless search that is the new work of the university.

The spreading of this idea over the course of the 19th and
20th centuries, as the new-model research university was elaborated and amalgamated with other models, laid the basis for
what seems self-evident now: namely, that in the university, the
rights of free speech have all the force they have in civil society
at large but a heightened value as well, as the preconditions for
the performance of the university's special work. But as soon as
it is said that the modern university claims free speech and free
inquiry as its foundational values, it must be added that this
value has always been contested, from outside the university
but also from within.

Why is this freedom always contested in practice, however
much it may be affirmed as an ideal? The question is almost too
simple: to be human is to know the answer. Both individually
and in groups, humans display traits at least as deep (in truth
far more primordial) than the desire to protect the freedom of
others. These would include the urge to intimidate others and
subject others to one's power—not an unknown trait even

among the liberally disposed and seemingly right-minded; and it would include less negative-sounding traits as well. It is of the nature of humans to hold values, and, within them, a differential range of values. These extend from mere preferences, things one would like to have but could stand to lose, to things taken to be of ultimate value, such that to dispute or cross them is felt as trespass, transgression, unacceptable to the last degree. Conviction, quite as much as insecurity or the will to power, is the breeding-ground of intolerance, fueling the notion that it is not only allowable to stop the transgressive thoughts and acts of others but a high exercise of virtue to do so.

As the place that claims to specialize in the creation of new thinking, the modern university will always attract both the special hopes and the special fears of the surrounding society, and as a home of both the play of curiosity and the desire to think rightly in the ethical sense, the modern university will always breed the energies of righteousness together with those of inquiry. In this light, it is not surprising that the modern university has been the prime scene both for the assertion of free speech and for major assaults on such freedom from both the right and the left, and we must not expect this tension to go away anytime soon. Yale's strong policy on free expression, articulated in the 1973 Woodward Report, speaks of "the right to think the unthinkable, discuss the unmentionable, and challenge the unchallengeable," and in the abstract, such rhetoric could lift every heart, somewhat in the manner of Superman's truth, freedom, and the American Way. But when others actually think what we find unthinkable and speak what we personally find unspeakable, the likely response will continue to be, That's unthinkable! You are unspeakable! So it is that universities are fated to host both free speech and various threats to this freedom, and doomed to the task of mediating between these conflicting forces.

If asked what the state of free speech is at this university today, I would reply that free speech is in a healthy state. We have not recently witnessed the sort of aggressive, self-righteous, community-wrenching assaults on this value that were seen, from one side, in the McCarthy era, or from the other, in attempted silencing of antiliberal speakers (at Yale, notably General William Westmoreland and the scientist or pseudoscientist William Shockley) on campus in the 1970s. More positively, this is nowadays a place where people feel generally free to pipe up and generally refrain from forcing their views on others in coercive ways. But the tensions and oppositions that free speech breeds have of course not gone away, and by my own diagnosis, they cannot be expected to. If there were no challenges to this value on campus, it could only mean that we were living in a state either of unimaginable docility or of unimaginable consensus — the tyranny of mutual agreement embodying a foe to free speech quite as damaging as any other. When I say that the state of free speech is healthy, then, I mean not that it is unproblematic but that it is problematic in a fairly healthy way. To give the flavor of the way issues present themselves and of the difficulties they pose, it might help to turn to some recent cases.

I have been dean for nine years. Never was there a year when school started more smoothly than this one. We had the freshmen arrive. It was lovely. We had freshman orientation. It was great. We went through the first weekend of school, when new students typically do stupid things they will eventually be too smart to do again. And we had almost no episodes of this sort. "What a year!" I might be pardoned for having thought. "This is going to be a piece of cake." Classes started on the fifth of September. The sixth was nice, and the seventh was nice, and the eighth was nice, and the ninth was nice. But then one morning, on September 11, 2001, out of the blue came the attack on the World Trade Center, an event that filled this campus, as it filled the country and much of the world, with anguish, terror, and uncertainty.

Right away, in the response, one saw admirable things about the fabric of the community. The administration, working with many helpers, pulled together a vigil to be held on Cross Campus that evening. Around 2,000 people attended, with every kind of person in the world standing side by side. It was a powerful experience, and President Levin spoke movingly about the importance of toleration at a time when it would be so tempting to scapegoat others. To me it was even more moving, two nights later, on the same plaza in front of Sterling Library, to come across a joint vigil organized by Jewish and Muslim students to show their respect for one another. One of the things one has to love about students is that they do not wait for the administration to make all the moves. These students took the initiative to put forth the image of a good community against a divisive threat. It was very, very admirable.

Within a day or two, there was discussion of the idea of holding a faculty panel to speak to issues the attack had blown open: Where had it come from? What did it mean? What future was it leading toward? What should be done? The idea was that, in a moment of horror and anguish, it might be especially valuable to bring some of the expertise of the university to bear, and so make this event an occasion for education.

I was included in the group that planned the panel, and I was eventually asked to be the moderator. Battell Chapel was secured for the event, and on Sunday evening, September 16, about 1,500 people gathered in this space, with a further 500 watching on closed-circuit television in the Law School Auditorium. We had, as is customary, assembled a group with varied expertise and points of view. Strobe Talbott, who had been Deputy Secretary of State in the Clinton administration, had just returned to Yale to head the Globalization Center. Talbott had been in government service when Al Qaeda had bombed the U.S.S. *Cole* and the embassy in Nairobi, so the "news" of 9/11 was not as new to him as to many. We also thought to ask our principal historian of the Muslim world, Abbas Amanat; also Paul Kennedy, the historian of the rise and fall of empires; also the economist Gus Ranis, who headed the Center for International and Area Studies; also the sociologist Deborah Davis, who was in close contact with students and faculty in China and could report a view from far away; and also Harold Koh of the Law School, who had just returned from a stint as Assistant Secretary for Democracy, Human Rights, and Labor in the State Department.

I went onstage with my colleagues, and after introducing the speakers I expected bloody battles to unfold. It was my understanding that the panel had sharply divergent views about the 9/11 assault, and I thought my skills as moderator would be heavily taxed. But strange to say, as the speakers made their separate statements, it was apparent that these people had undergone a strange convergence. I had put Strobe Talbott first and Abbas Amanat second because Talbott had spoken of being troubled by things Amanat had written in a *Yale Daily News* editorial. They would give a punch and counterpunch, I expected — but as they spoke, they had modulated their differences and converged toward common ground, as later speakers did as well.

Third came Paul Kennedy, who asked the audience to engage in a thought experiment. Why do they hate us? he asked. What would explain the mental state of a person who wanted to fly airplanes into tall American buildings and kill thousands of people? Well, what would it be like to live at a time when America was dominant everywhere and in every sphere and you were not a beneficiary of American power? What if you felt that America was putting values in global circulation that were deeply antithetical to your own values? And on he went. To stay within the time limit, Kennedy was the only person who had written out his remarks, and his having done so meant that his thoughts were expressed with powerful eloquence and economy. When he finished, the whole of Battell Chapel applauded, which induced in me (and likely too in Paul) a considerable discomfort. People clap for a position statement or a piece of advocacy, and none of us was there for that. We were there to explore the meaning of a devastating and difficult experience from different sides — the panel was meant to illustrate what Justice Learned Hand meant when he said that "right conclusions are more likely to be gathered out of a multitude of tongues, than through any kind of authoritative selection." We did not expect, and we did not wish, the experience of unanimity.

It was in many ways a good event, certainly an edifying one, but it left me with the vague sense that something had not worked out as planned. So I was not wholly surprised that in the days that followed, the panel was blasted — harshly attacked by students and some distinguished faculty members for its suppression of other points of view. The panel was attacked for accepting the notion that America was somehow to blame for the 9/11 assault. It was also attacked for not including anyone to say that, so far from needing to be "understood," the deed should be denounced as simply evil, and future attacks defended against in the most aggressive fashion.

Soon enough the nature of the problem became clear. We had held an event for the sake of education. We had planned it as an exercise of multiple points of view, in keeping with Learned Hand's wisdom that "it is only by crosslights from varying directions that full illumination can be secured." But it turned out that the event had been at best a partial fulfillment of this aspiration, and in the eyes of some, a failure or worse: an event in which some points of view were rehearsed again and again, and others denied the chance for expression.

This is a classic example of free speech and its vicissitudes in the university. As I review the criticisms in retrospect, I would make a number of points. First, it is uncharitable to hold anyone to the notion that on September 16, 2001, they should have known exactly what to say. This was a painful and confusing time. The size of the death toll was still not established. No one knew if another terrorist attack was imminent. No one knew if the United States would be dropping bombs somewhere across the world by the time we came out of the chapel that night. In charity, we need to allow each other some margin for error at such a trying time.

Second, to the extent that there was a degree of homogeneity on the panel, it was completely unintended. The panel had been structured with the understanding that it would articulate serious differences, but those differences failed to emerge. As an organizer of a panel, one can only do so much. If you ask people to speak and you want them to think aloud rather than "stand for" fixed positions in quasi-allegorical manner, you are at the mercy of their freedom — their freedom to choose their own words.

Further, if there was a failure of inclusiveness on the panel, and I do not deny that there was in some measure, in effect if not in intent, the remedy was at hand. People could denounce the event and express the temporarily neglected points of view, and they hastened to do so. Editorials flew in the *Yale Daily News* and indeed in the national media. (The media's virulent distortion of Paul Kennedy into a kind of apologist for terror, as if he had said that because terrorism had causes it was therefore morally justified, gave its own education in the powers of intimidation and assault.)

If a point of view had been missing, therefore, it was not so systematically suppressed that it did not become available quickly thereafter, and with important results. Some people always know what they think about everything, but many felt their received understandings to have been powerfully punctured by the events of 9/11. This was perhaps especially true of undergraduates, for whom that day represented an altogether new order of experience. All of us need education all our lives, but students need education even more, because they are young. How many pre–9/11 undergraduates should we suppose had ever had a serious, visceral occasion to think about the moral conditions that justify war, or about the nature of security—where it comes from, how fully it can be achieved, and what costs it might justify and exact? In my view, the business of the university at this ghastly time was to provide the wherewithal for education. Not to tell students what to think, which is never the business of the university, but to give free play to a range of thoughtful responses against which students could test their own understandings and build their own thoughtful sense of things. Within days, I believe, such a range was available on campus, and we could all go about the work of reflection.

The next Friday, at lunchtime, I was sitting in my office when a student bolted in. The door of my office is usually open, and people just run in sometimes. (This actually happens not too rarely.) This student, who was literally quivering with indignation, presented me with a poster she had found on the street. It showed an American flag, depicted in colors extremely washed out and pallid, across which was printed the slogan: "These Colors Do Run" — an ironic inversion of the old chauvinistic bumper sticker that boasted "These Colors Don't Run." But then, crudely scrawled across the poster, was the object of the student's wrath. (It is repugnant to me to repeat this, but I can't re-create the difficulty of this situation unless I do so). This was the word "sandnigger." In my innocence, I did not know this term — I was quickly informed that it was an anti-Muslim slur — though I needed no education to see that it was the ugliest kind of word, a denigration of one group made by reviving the denigration of another. The student demanded that I issue a statement denouncing the poster and see that the person who posted it was punished.

In a university, free speech issues usually come up with no advance notice, and have to be responded to with a kind of improvisatory wisdom. On the spot, called on to make an official reply to an event I had now known of for as long as 30 seconds, I had the following thoughts. First, I could see why the student was indignant. This was an act of rank, unmitigated bigotry. Such bigotry is offensive for its brutality but also for its stupidity: to think that people can be known by linking them to abstract categories, about which one knows absolutely nothing except by way of prejudice, is a total failure of intelligence, as also of charity. In the university, the presence of such bigotry is both a social and an intellectual offense, and this scrawl was particularly offensive in the circumstances of its time. That very year, Yale had enrolled by far the largest number of international students we had ever had in an entering class, in the first class to profit from need-blind admission for foreign applicants. So we had significant numbers of new students from places like Pakistan, Turkey, and Malaysia. It was particularly appalling to think that these young people would have come halfway around the world, to a strange new land they had now inhabited for two weeks, only to find themselves the objects of denigration or hatred.

Nevertheless, when it was put to me that I should do something about the poster, there were also other facts to weigh.

First and most obviously, it was an anonymous act. We had no way to know who had posted it, or even, since it was found on a city street, whether it was the work of a student at all. Beyond that, I had problems with the notion that the Dean should step forward to denounce it. One concern was prudential: if an official begins circulating mass e-mails decrying every act of incivility in the community, the effect would be that all such messages would soon go unnoticed. But my real concern was of a deeper sort. As I saw it, to say that the Dean must officially decry this instance was to imply that the institution must undertake to be the enforcer of proper speech, on campus on all occasions. (It does, of course, when a true disciplinary offense is involved.) And I saw problems with that notion.

First, I believe that the university must think many times before it allows itself to be enlisted in the work of silencing, even when the thing silenced is abhorrent. When universities get in the business of suppressing speech, however vile, it lends credence to the notion that it is a legitimate function of the university to suppress speech. A notion is thereby validated that can then be activated on a later occasion—perhaps to suppress one's own dissident or unpopular expression.

Second, I asked myself: if a condemnation is to be made, and I never doubted that one was appropriate, was it really the case that it would be better for the Dean, and not the young woman herself, to condemn the thing? When I put this question, the student replied, unsurprisingly, "If you say it, it carries more weight." To this I replied that the power of this weapon is easily overstated—messages from the Dean lose force in proportion to their frequency—and that for me to do what she requested was to embrace the notion that it was the Dean's job and nobody else's to say, instance by instance, why offensive things are offensive. University officials have a role in this regard and I have not hesitated to play it, but it is my strong conviction that there must never be an administrative monopoly on this function. The moral order of the university community is everyone's business and everyone's responsibility to uphold and create. These are not matters they should take care of at headquarters. They are issues every community member has a stake in and the power to act on. To delegate them to some official to deal with is to weaken the sense of individual duty and power. I urged the student to write an editorial or seek other ways to speak her own views. In doing so, I had one further thought in mind as well.

Condemnation and censure have their place in a university, and punishment can and should be exacted for a serious offense. But in a university setting, these can never be the preferred mode of response. The machinery of condemnation and punishment nails the offender to the category "guilty" or "morally defective person." But in universities of all places, people need to work from the notion that others and even they themselves are teachable: capable of recognizing their limitations (even moral limitations) and passing out from them to a more enlightened state. We need to help each other to this enlightenment, so we all must take the roles by turns of teacher and of student. For the young woman to think of the person who scrawled the epithet as capable of education, and for her herself to undertake the work of explanation and persuasion, would have been, I thought, a good outcome to a bad case.

Let me add another thing. This student could not know that the day before, another undergraduate, this one too a total stranger, had also come to my office unannounced, to complain that a teacher had made derogatory remarks about the American military in a lecture. She found this offensive at this alarming time because her father was in the army. It occurs to me that if this woman had seen the poster the other student complained of, she too might have felt wounded—but by the message "These Colors Do Fade," with its casual wish of ill to the nation and its military. Taken together, these episodes taught me that one person's self-satisfied slogan is another's hurtful jab, and that the more sensitive we are to our own offended state, the more unlikely we are to realize the possibly different offenses suffered by others. I listened to this woman with sympathy and told her that, in my view, what she should do is go up to the teacher and explain to him how his remarks had registered from her point of view—not accusingly, but with the thought that this might never have occurred to him. She told me that that was just what she had done.

I will mention one more episode from this time and then I will conclude. On the following Sunday evening, giving in to a bad habit, I decided to read my e-mail before going to bed. It included a message from a freshman counselor reporting that a banner had been hung from a freshman room on the Old Campus blaring the message: "Kill Them All. Let God sort them out." The counselor found the message objectionable, as well he might. When I wrote back to urge persuasion as the best tactic for the case, I learned that he had needed no such lesson. He had already written a statement to the campus paper: had already stepped out of the easily deadlocked logic of offense and accusation to do the different work of a potential educator.

But the story, alas, did not end there. The next day, word reached me that other freshman counselors had taken down the banner or urged the student to do so. They did so, I never doubted, out of no self-righteous or censorious motives but to do what they were there for: to promote mutual respect in a community of very various people who were still nearly strangers. But this apparently reasonable action was in fact deeply unacceptable. As I by now was getting good at explaining, since the counselors were agents of the Dean, their removal of the banner was tantamount to an institutional suppression of speech. (It would of course have been only marginally less problematic if they had done it on their own.) And the university should be reluctant to license the suppression of any speech, however objectionable, lest it validate the notion that that speech is something right to suppress. By the end of this day, I found myself in the morally peculiar position of requesting the counselors to restore the offending banner. (These were, I repeat, strange times.) By this point, however, the banner's maker—who claimed, in any case, that the saying did not mean what it was being taken to mean and was a quotation from an old song—had no further wish to display it.

Now I ask myself: how were the counselors to know what

was right to do? These were admirable, generous-minded, thoughtful people who took the responsibilities of their position very seriously. (It was excruciating to seem to fault them.) But they were in their very early 20s and in the middle of a national emergency: what training or prior experience could have taught them exactly what weight to give to the conflicting moral imperatives they found themselves subjected to? I return to a point I made before: in a university, as also in the larger world, it is wrong to act as if everyone should always already know just what is right to do. In daily practice, the domain of free speech issues is a world of deep moral difficulty, where values clash with other compelling values in novel and unfamiliar combinations, and where finding the right balance can tax the wisest head. Since this is so, we need to allow ourselves and others some space in face of these conflicts: some room to work through to the understanding we may not at first possess. In short, we need to allow free speech and its vicissitudes to be a scene of education.

This brings me to my conclusion. I am a peaceable person. I have no love of conflict; to the contrary. But experiences like the ones I have recounted—and any month or year could furnish its own materials—have taught me, first, that the university will never be a conflict-free zone; and second, that we should not wish for this even if it were obtainable. Free speech is a resonant ideal, but we only learn the meaning of the value when it is put to the test—or rather, when we are put to the test, in situations of painful and confusing ethical conflict. I would never have chosen for any of these events to have occurred. But when they did happen, they made powerful chapters of education: education for individual students, whose awareness of the difficulties of the ethical was enriched through these trials; education for the larger community; and education not least for me. It cannot be the work of universities to insulate free speech from all possible assault. But it can be their work to protect this freedom in extensive ways. And above all, it should be their work to make the attendant struggles a chance to learn—to win deeper understanding of our values, why we hold them, and how they require us to act.

THE NEW INTERNATIONALISM
GLOBALIZING COMPARATIVE LITERATURE

All contemporary American universities are involved in the self-conscious process of internationalizing themselves. This talk, the keynote address from a conference of Yale and Chinese scholars on "Globalizing Comparative Literature," gives a history of this process's dynamics and challenges through the lens of one discipline. Delivered at Tsinghua University, Beijing, August 11, 2001.

I AM A PROFESSOR of literature, but for the past eight years I have worked in the administration of my university, and this has yielded losses and gains. On the one hand, I have been much less involved in my own projects and the state of play in my discipline. In compensation, my "day" job has given me a clearer sense of the university as a whole and how it has shaped itself in response to a changing world. My colleagues will deliver the intellectual goods you came for, but I hope you will pardon me if I address our topic from this more distanced perspective. With your permission, I want to sketch my sense of how the global turn in Comparative Literature fits into the evolving organization of university study.

The phrase "Globalizing Comparative Literature" suggests a new thing being done to an old or established discipline. More particularly, "globalizing" suggests the spread to Comparative Literature of—or the discipline's wish to annex itself to—a process whose more famous home is well outside literary study. With amazing rapidity, the new term "globalization" has become the accepted shorthand name for the central development of the contemporary world, a multisided transformation driven from several different domains. On the one hand, globalization names the technological revolution that has brought hundreds of millions of people into touch with each other in a communications network that annihilates geographical distance and political boundaries. (I have read that 300,000 additional people gain access to the Internet every week.) On another front, globalization describes the increasing interdependence of economic systems and financial markets, the process by which once relatively separate economies have been integrated into the free market and come to share in its dynamisms and instabilities. On yet another front, globalization is a development in which culture itself has become an import-export business and a streaming technology. In the contemporary world, social practices and signifying forms that once belonged somewhere and expressed some particular people have been unmoored and put in global circulation, to be imaginatively inhabited or (as we say) "entertained" in the swirling succession of foods, films, musics, and styles of modern everyday life.

There is much to say about globalization, but the first thing to say is that the process is hardly new. Everyone will have a favorite example of cross-global interaction in the days before globalization. Since I am working on a study of the American prophetic tradition, the radical self-assertions produced by people who have laid claim to visionary authority, I would call to mind the fact that Joseph Smith, the prophet-founder of the Church of Jesus Christ of Latter Day Saints, which currently claims 10 million members worldwide, grew up in poverty because his parents, who lived in a remote area of one of America's most rural regions, in Vermont, were ruined around 1800 by their misguided investments in the ginseng trade with China. For an example on the Chinese side, my colleague Jonathan Spence has shown that in the prehistory of the 1850s' Taiping Rebellion, one of the ingredients that fed Hong Xiuquan's explosive fantasy that he was a new messianic incarnation or God's Chinese son was a religious pamphlet transmitted through a Yale graduate doing missionary work along the

Chinese coast—so little is it true that distant cultures have only now begun to interpenetrate and interact. But if globalization is not new, the inclusiveness, speed, and depth of contemporary interactions are new, and we can discriminate this process's phases even as we recognize its continuities.

Comparative Literature is a study in which objects elsewhere seen as belonging to separate national traditions are grasped instead in a relational way. Comparative Literature is thus an intercultural discipline, but it is also the product of an intercultural history, and the turns of its evolution reflect the changing forms of exchange that have taken place within and around universities. Let me offer a pocket history of Comparative Literature at Yale as an index to the course of these transformations.

Nowhere in history has the university ever been an indigenous institution. Universities have never sprung from merely local causes or been built with purely local ideas. Their structures and ambitions have always been translations, re-creations in a new place of ideas carried across linguistic and political boundaries. The medieval universities fashioned at Bologna, then Paris, then Oxford and Cambridge were so many importations of a portable idea, whose replication wove a culture of learning across widely separate geographical locales.

The idea of the university entered what is now the United States (as it arguably entered China) through the cultural transfer mechanisms of European colonialism. The first colleges in America were founded by English immigrants who remembered the educational institutions of their home. Since the religion of the New England colonists gave central cultural importance to a learned clergy, they felt an urgent need to equip their new home with an appropriate training ground, founding institutions of higher learning while their settlements were in every way peripheral and underdeveloped. The Massachusetts Puritans founded their new Cambridge and erected its frontier college—Harvard—in 1636, or within six years of their arrival in Boston. When Yale was founded as a second New England college in 1701, the colony of Connecticut has a total population not exceeding 30,000.

It would be impossible to overestimate the extent to which foreign languages and writings in foreign tongues – what we might call proto–Comparative Literature – were the centerpiece of the first American universities. Students could enter early Yale at any age when they had sufficient preparation in Classical languages, and they spent their college years perfecting their Greek and Latin, reading Cicero and Virgil and the Greek New Testament. These colleges were places of access to the foreign, in other words, but the scope and content of this foreignness were delimited by the educational paradigm that informed them: one blending a medieval Classical curriculum since accepted as the proper education of the elite with a special Protestant emphasis on Biblical scholarship. (By this logic, it will not surprise you to learn that the first new language regularly offered at Yale was Old Testament Hebrew.) Shortly after the American Revolution, Noah Webster, a Yale graduate of the 1780s and the compiler of the first American dictionary, published a plan for a distinctively American scheme of education in which future merchants would learn the languages of contemporary commerce, not useless ancient tongues. This was for many years a dissident view but it reinforces my larger point: no language has ever been offered in a university except in conjunction with some cultural program that marked that language as valuable to know.

Modern languages and literature in its modern, secular forms entered the field of study at Yale in the 19th century. But such subjects entered the curriculum not through some natural growth or dawning recognition of their inevitable interest but through new cross-cultural collisions that forced deep changes in the philosophy of education. Later in the 19th century, as American colleges liberalized and to some extent secularized their original religious mission, literary study got a boost from an Anglophile embrace of humanism in the manner of Matthew Arnold, who argued that literature could fill the void as a source or ground of value in a postreligious age. Somewhat earlier, American education had its eyes turned from the ancient British universities to Germany. German universities had pioneered the break with traditional Classics-centered instruction and introduced the study of modern subjects (for instance history) in the 18th century. Building on these changes, Wilhelm von Humboldt laid down the structures of a new model university, the prototype of the modern research university, in Berlin in the 1810s. By the 1830s these new centers had sufficiently established their prestige that Americans began to look to Germany as the capital of the academic world and to head to German universities as the place for postgraduate training. (By the logic of this moment it was natural for the African-American scholar W. E. B. DuBois — who would eventually die in the then unheard-of Ghana — to go to Berlin to do doctoral work in Philosophy). Such scholars brought home the new ideas of education they had learned abroad. These ideas, which included a far more specialized ideal of professorial expertise, a new hierarchy of faculty positions keyed to specialized research accomplishment, and a new hierarchy of student roles — especially the creation of separate graduate study — for the training of specialized intelligence, were gradually incorporated into existing American institutions, producing the hybrid blend of aims and structures that is the American university.

Literary study as we know it — the study of modern, not ancient, and secular, not sacred, texts — got its foothold in American universities through these developments. But it did not enter the curriculum in an unconditioned way. Having been promoted by these larger revisions in the idea of education, literary study was shaped in their image and instituted on their terms. If we look at the American university as it emerged in the late 19th and early 20th centuries (this holds true really into the 1940s), we would find literary study taking these forms: the study of Classical literature perpetuated from the first plan of the university; side by side with this, the study of modern languages and literatures conducted in the Germanic scholarly mode, with heavy emphasis on historical philology and textual scholarship; and a post-Arnoldian humanistic study that dealt with secular imaginative writing (principally poetry), but in ways that would strike us as amateurish or belletristic.

The change from this establishment to literary study as we know it was the result of another deep reconstruction involving further cross-national collisions. The transformation of these older American schools into the international academic research centers of the present has its roots in the social disruptions of the mid-20th century, especially the rise of fascism and Communism and the World War and Cold War they produced. As you know, the United States emerged from World War II taking itself far more seriously as a potential world leader, an idea the Cold War hardened into a national mission. At this time, the role academic (particularly scientific) expertise had played in the winning of the war led to a new recognition of the universities' centrality to national eminence and power, so that starting in the late 1940s, new levels of both ambition and funding began to be invested in higher education and university research. Fatefully, just as American universities raised their ambitions at this time, they were able to recruit a new kind of faculty member to realize the new intellectual level: European scholars uprooted by the European social crises. René Wellek is a classic example. Born in Vienna of a Czech father and a Polish-Prussian-Swiss mother, raised in the new nation Czechoslovakia, if Wellek had lived in a more peaceful world he might have spent his career in Prague, or Vienna, or conceivably even Berlin. But developments in Central Europe in the 1930s drove him to exile in England, from which he was lured to an American academic post at Iowa—from which Yale, flush with the new internationalist ambitions of the postwar years, recruited him in 1949.

Comparative Literature was officially founded at Yale with the arrival of René Wellek. Yale's first Professor of Comparative Literature, Wellek was appointed into a department that was created for his hiring. Other recruits to the new discipline were products of the same intellectual diaspora. Erich Auerbach, whose *Mimesis* is one of the great comparative literary studies ever written, left Hitler's Germany to find refuge in Turkey, where *Mimesis* was composed. There was no returning to Germany after the war, and Auerbach found a new scholarly home in

America—first for one year at Princeton, then as Professor of Romance Languages at Yale. Other new arrivals around 1950, the Comparative Literature Department's first graduate students, had similar origins. Geoffrey Hartman was born in Germany but fled Nazism to England and then the United States. Peter Demetz, who like Hartman would become a great Professor of Comparative Literature at Yale in his turn, had fled both the Nazis and the Russians in his departure from Czechoslovakia.

These émigré trajectories brought Yale a faculty that taught with foreign accents and thought in foreign idioms. Since they had contact with distant intellectual cultures, these figures subjected Yale and the American intellectual world to a powerful deprovincialization, bringing modes of inquiry from avant-garde Europe to new mental life in the United States. With his immense erudition in all the European critical traditions, René Wellek was a great incarnation of the Germanic-style encyclopedic scholar, but Wellek also knew Roman Jakobson and was conversant with the Russian formalists, and the book that led to his hiring at Yale — *Theory of Literature*, co-authored with Austin Warren (1949) — gave American currency to this alien thought. When such imports were joined with America's home-grown theoretical movement the New Criticism, exemplified at Yale by such figures as William Wimsatt, Cleanth Brooks, and Robert Penn Warren, the result was to make "theory" a part of literary study in an altogether new way—in other words, to change the whole nature of literary reflection.

From this beginning in the postwar world Comparative Literature developed the features of its modern life. Comp Lit became a kind of foreign recruitment center, attracting a succession of brilliant émigrés—Paul de Man and Shoshana Felman would be later recruits—and native-born students with international contacts and perspectives. (When J. Hillis Miller came to Yale in 1972, he was known both for his critical work on Victorian literature and his connections to the Geneva School.) The faculty thus assembled was sometimes yoked together as "the Yale School," but there was nothing uniform about the way they did their work. They were united instead by habits of mind rooted in the history I have traced. Competent in many languages and deeply schooled in their literatures, these figures were adepts at close reading, but they crossbred this rather static method with a continual infusion of new paradigms from Europe — Structuralism, Derridian philosophy, Freudian and Lacanian psychoanalysis, the works of Foucault and Bakhtin, French feminism, and the rest — designed to theorize and so to speak volatilize interpretation. In the work that resulted, criticism and theory fused and transformed each other, with imported extraliterary paradigms supplying a new horizon for literary interpretation and the reading of literary works giving the means to test the power of larger models. Comp Lit became not so much a way to study writing as a way to engage in thinking — a mode of thinking always straining to win deepened self-consciousness for the acts of reading and interpretation.

But when premodern versions of Comparative Literature gave intellectual play to the foreign, they did so within constraints; and this was true of postwar Comparative Literature as well. Like its predecessors, this disciplinary formation mapped the world in the image of its founding values, inviting exchange in some directions but neglecting or unconsciously blocking it in others. The first thing that could be called Comparative Literature at Yale included in its relevant "world" Greek, Latin, and to a lesser extent Hebrew. While maintaining residual loyalty to these older languages and cultures, Comparative Literature of the 1950s through the 1980s found its centers in the seats of modern European scholarship and the scenes of the intellectual diaspora — Germany, France, to some extent Italy, to some extent Russia: a differently delimited horizon but still a delimited one. Not surprisingly, given the new role that Asia played in United States history in the 1940s and early 1950s, Yale already offered high-level training in Asian history and literatures by the 1950s, but Yale Comparative Literature did not teach Asian subjects or cross-appoint scholars of Chinese or Japanese literature. (It is telling that Thomas Greene, the great scholar of the classics and the European Renaissance and René Wellek's successor as the Chair of Comparative Literature, studied Japanese in the 1940s in the U.S. Army but did not continue it when he entered the new Department of Comp Lit as a graduate student—for the obvious reason that Asia was not part of Comp Lit's operative universe.) Quite as revealing of these invisible boundaries, Spanish, though a European language, scarcely figured in the linguistic universe of Comparative Literature either, meaning that Latin America too was consigned to terra incognita.

If this situation has changed, and our presence here declares that it has, it has not been from mere natural growth or inevitable progress. This change has resulted from another revision of the force field that has been brought to bear on universities: what I might half-facetiously call The Fourth Internationalization. There is not time to name all the factors that have made schools like Yale aware of the limits of their earlier internationalism and eager to open themselves to the world. The increased scale of modern economic, political, and environmental interdependence, which has supplemented the United States' traditional ties to Europe with equally powerful links with other parts of the world, is the most obvious contributing cause. But modern migration patterns and changes in American immigration laws have had this effect as well. While a generation ago virtually every American university was peopled with native-born students or students of European extraction, in the wake of modern migrations American colleges have more and more outstanding students whose parents emigrated from China, or India, or Vietnam, or Turkey, or Mexico, or the Dominican Republic. Given the interconnection of research activities at major universities around the world (especially in the sciences), and with the fall of political barriers that had blocked the free flow of intelligence, the graduate student population in current American universities is more international still. This new, more diversified mobility has pressed a more globalized image on every aspect of contemporary culture. If American cultural imports in China are becoming bizarrely more natural by the day, it's quite as "natural" that one of the most successful current American filmmakers should be Ang Lee (what a world in which a Chinese filmmaker should become the principal interpreter of the most deeply British of all writers — Jane Austen — to the American popular audience!), or that one of the most interesting recent American novelists should be Ha Jin (Xuefei Jin), who came to the U.S. from the P.R.C. as a graduate student in 1985. Given the new academic demographics, universities have become particularly active centers for this wider cultural exchange.

The very strength with which it incorporated the postwar model of internationalism meant that, at Yale as at most American universities, Comparative Literature was not in the vanguard of this wider internationalization. But Comp Lit has moved in this direction in the last 10 or 15 years to the extent that it has now virtually reinvented itself on a globalist model. I well remember one of the early steps in this history. When I was the Chair of the English Department, I believe the year was 1989, the English Department joined Comparative Literature in inviting the Kenyan novelist and critic Ngugi wa Thiong'o to Yale as a Visiting Professor. Though the word was not yet in use, this was clearly a globalizing move, a move to reach out of literary study's Anglo-European confines, reflecting the growing interest in the postcolonial in the American academy in the 1980s. In the modern way of things, to reach a Kenyan novelist we wrote to London, where Ngugi was living in exile. When he arrived in New Haven (we had not received advance word that he was coming), he came by way of New York, Stockholm, and Botswana, where he had been writing a journalistic piece on commission (if I remember right) for a German magazine. Ngugi was at this time famous for his anticolonialist polemics in *Decolonising the Mind,* and when he arrived in the United States he had renounced the literary use of English in favor of his tribal language. In consequence, in the memorable spring terms of 1990 and 1991, diagonally across the street from the Comparative Literature library, with its thousands of volumes in Latin, English, German, and French, Ngugi sat typing plays and filmscripts in what had suddenly become a new language of

Yale Comparative Literature: Gikuyu. As Ngugi recalls in the essay "Life, Literature and a Longing for Home" in the collection *Moving the Centre*, when the editors of the then-new *Yale Journal of Criticism* asked him for a submission, he hoped to escape by replying that he only wrote in Gikuyu, but the editor (Sara Suleri) "looked me in the eye and said: write in Gikuyu. We shall publish it." Which they did — with facing translations, to be sure.

Ngugi's teaching gave Yale a taste of what he called "moving the centre," but in 1990 there was still something quite exceptional, if also extraordinarily powerful, about Ngugi's presence as a colleague. By contrast, in recent years the move out and away from the Eurocentric has become less the exception and more the norm. In a series of recent steps, Yale's undergraduate Comparative Literature program has devised an experimental course in World Literature co-taught by people whose expertise runs from ancient Assyrian to Indian diasporic writing in South Africa. A new Yale Professor of Comparative Literature, recruited like Wellek from Iowa, Dudley Andrew, one of the founders of the discipline of Film Studies, started his work on French Cinema but now extends his range through most of the cinematic cultures of the world. In a move to my mind long overdue, the professors of Comparative Literature have discovered a community of interest with Yale's equally distinguished professors of East Asian Literature, as exemplified in the partnership here today of Michael Holquist and Kang-i Chang. Our newest senior recruit, if we have the luck to land him, will be a person versed in both Chinese literature and the Classical literature of the West, and at home not just in Western theory but in its contemporary Eastern translations and adaptations. Broadening the community yet further, we now seek conversation partners from far and wide — which brings us here to Tsinghua.

It is not in my power to say what the content will be of the globalized Comparative Literature that we are obviously moving toward. We are here not to proclaim some new disciplinary consensus but to explore the possibilities together. But as I prepare to quit the role of speaker in this dialogue to take up the more interesting role of listener, I would say three quick things about the place we have reached.

First and most obviously, globalizing Comparative Literature is easier said than done. Students of literature (of all people) should know how much the meaning of any message lies in the way it activates the whole system of a language, its full play of tonalities and allusions and implications. It was already not easy to learn three or four languages to the point of being able to appreciate what was lost in translation. But if globalizing Comparative Literature is not in practice to mean trivializing Comparative Literature, reducing it to what a marketer would call Comp Lit Lite, then we had better be prepared to learn more languages and learn them well. I take note of how very easy it is for me to speak in China since you understand English and speak English back. There is, I know, one view in which such asymmetrical conversation is the very triumph of globalization. Especially in the United States, there are many who think that what globalization means is the coming happy interdependence of the whole world within a magically internationalized Americanism, where "we" will be able to enjoy the foreignness of things all the more since they really won't be very foreign at all. But it is a well-known paradox that contemporary globalization sponsors both the homogenization of cultures and the reproduction of local cultural differences, so we should not be betting that the "we're-all-connected" world will be a world without linguistic difference. In any case, true students of Comparative Literature will want to be the connoisseurs of verbal and cultural differences and of the continual negotiations among them.

Second, as Comparative Literature begins its globalizing phase, it needs to be wary of an implicit conceptual hegemony that would be quite as impoverishing as a linguistic one. Comp Lit will have globalized itself one way, but not perhaps in the most interesting way, if it can enlist a cross-national community in using an academic discourse marked Made in America and framing questions the same way we do. I do not fantasize that the different world cultures should each have their own indigenous Comparative Literature. Everything interesting that has ever been achieved in Comparative Literature has come from the traffic in foreign-born ideas and their redeployment on new grounds. But we will have the most valuable version of the coming exchange if we allow the trade in understanding to be truly open and multilateral: if we are as willing to recognize the power of foreign conceptualizations as to insist on the preeminence of our own, if we are as willing to learn as to teach.

Last, as it proceeds through its impending transformation, Comparative Literature needs to think about what the discipline has to offer to a globalizing world. Next to the great engines of mass culture and finance and technology, academic literary study seems a fairly marginal shaper of the current age. Those of us who practice this study do so in the conviction that it connects us to a power of understanding not obtainable through other means. But we cannot assume that others will feel this power if we do not take the trouble to project it. Comp Lit in the past generation had an intellectual presence out of all proportion to any known interest in the art of literary interpretation because it developed the sense that there was something it grasped that was undeniably real and not otherwise easily thought about: the necessity of interpretation to meaning and the indeterminacy interpretation inevitably confers on meaning. The discipline will have comparable standing in the future in proportion as it evolves a comparably deep understanding for a newer world. "Globalizing Comparative Literature" *could* mean not just internationalizing the discipline's reading list or the directory of its practitioners but making Comparative Literature a lens for the sharper viewing of globalization: the tool through which transfers across cultures could be tracked and the nature of their interactions theoretically modeled.

In any case, we have come here not to say what a globalized Comparative Literature is but to begin to ask what it might be. We from Yale come in hopes that we have something to teach and in the certainty that we have much to learn. Above all, we come in confidence that, whatever globalized Comparative Literature may turn out to be, it will be the product of no one place or party but of a widespread dialogue among the thoughtful and intelligent. At your kind invitation, we have come halfway around the world to have some conversation with you. As Ezra Pound wrote in his poem to Walt Whitman, "Let there be commerce between us."

OFFICIAL BUSINESS

REMARKS ON
THE TERCENTENNIAL OF
YALE UNIVERSITY

The 300th anniversary of the founding of Yale was celebrated in a
yearlong program of activities that culminated in a grand ceremony
held in front of Sterling Library on October 6, 2001. On this occasion,
I was asked to speak on behalf of the faculty. This gave an occasion
to reflect on the university in time: to look back to the long past, and
forward to a long future.

THREE HUNDRED YEARS: this place is getting seriously old!
In fact the school that once dipped its stones in acidic baths to
give them an air of antiquity begins to be as old as it once
wished to seem! How are we to think of this amassing antiquity? One effect of Yale's tercentennial is to underscore how
little time any of us spends thinking about Yale's history, and by
my lights, this is not a failure. Though they also conserve the
past, universities exist to supply knowledge for the future
world, and their natural look is ahead, not behind. But this
day's anniversary invites us to see Yale in the light of history's
long extensions, so I hope it's pardonable if, for two or three
minutes every hundred years, we take a backward glance.

One of the great agents and products of globalization, a
process that began more than 10 years ago, the university has
always had the character of an imported good. Like their successors now found in every part of the globe, the medieval universities fashioned at Bologna, then Paris, then Oxford and
Cambridge were translations, re-creations in new places of an
idea carried across political and linguistic bounds. The idea of

the university crossed the Atlantic with the English immigrants to New England, who attached a value far beyond nostalgia to the schools of their youth. This group's religion assigned central importance to the idea of a learned clergy, so they went right to work building a place where the needed training could be supplied. The Massachusetts Puritans founded their new Cambridge and erected the frontier college Harvard within six years of their arrival in Boston. When Yale was founded as a second New England college in 1701, the colony of Connecticut had a total population not exceeding 30,000.

Being human, the founders of this place had a mix of motives. They were actuated in part by the desire to spare the expense of travel to distant Cambridge for their children's education. They also wanted to create a school that would transmit a severe religious orthodoxy, since by their lights Harvard had become a spiritual cesspool and scene of creeping open-mindedness. But their dominant motive, we must suppose, was that of anyone who founds a college or university. They wanted to create a place where the things humans have succeeded in understanding could be preserved and expanded, and where the young could be prepared for constructive lives in the world.

Given the vicissitudes of its rather fly-by-night early years, it's a wonder that this school outlived its infancy. The Collegiate School (as Yale was first called) first met in the home of a pastor in a settlement so remote that the 13 students threatened to run away. When this first rector died, the school limped along without a leader for nearly a decade, during which time this tiny operation literally disintegrated into three geographically separate fragments. When Yale was finally reunited in New Haven and amassed funds to build its first building, its stability was assured. But no one of that time would have had the least ability to imagine what Yale has since become. The tiny provincial academy has grown into one of the great modern research universities, and the place that taught a handful of young men from the surrounding area now draws gifted men and women from every sector of this country and the world. But though no surface feature of modern Yale would be recognizable to Yale's founders, and while many features would almost certainly appall them, what we're here to do is unchanged at bottom: to expand the reach of knowledge, and to give people of promise that exercise of their powers that will help them make thoughtful, constructive contributions to the life of their times.

Today I have the honor to speak as a representative of the faculty. In my experience, faculty members prefer to speak for themselves, but I trust I speak for many when I say that this occasion makes us mindful of the privileges our work lets us take for granted. To be a member of this faculty is to be not only licensed but even rewarded for following our private curiosities, encouraged to pursue questions that are compelling to our minds whether the great world sees their interest or not— though as recent weeks have shown, areas of expertise that have seemed hopelessly arcane can suddenly prove to shed light on matters of deep public concern. To be of this faculty is to have the highest quality support for our research, and no less crucially, to teach at Yale is to enjoy continual access to the stimulation that makes thinking happen: the company of smart colleagues, easily enjoyed at a place where bounds of disciplines and schools are easily crossed, and the company of students who care about their education and are engaged and creative enough to push our inquiries in new directions, and so become partners in the creation of knowledge.

But if the tercentennial's long view teaches anything, it's that the conditions we enjoy did not come from nowhere. Everything we take for granted is available to us because someone, at some earlier time, saw the need for it and took the trouble to bring it into being. For that reason, as we enjoy our freedoms, it must be part of our work to take the pains in our day that will let the University give maximum benefit to future users. I'm vaguely glad that Yale is old, but I'm extremely glad that "old" isn't the most interesting thing Yale is, and a tercentennial would be cause for embarrassment and sorrow if this school's great days did not lie ahead far more than they lie behind. They will lie ahead in proportion as all who love Yale continue to work to find new ways to pursue our goals in history's changing situations. To know that we receive the work of enlightened predecessors is to be reminded that it is for us too to do the work of founders: to use our powers, in our day, to make this a place of free and lively mental exploration, open to people of talent and commitment from every background, where human understanding can be cared for, and worked toward, and shared, and renewed.

SELECTIONS FROM THE
REPORT ON YALE
COLLEGE EDUCATION

The Report on Yale College Education was the culmination of a year-and-a-half self-study commissioned at the time of the Yale tercentennial. This was the most extensive review of Yale's undergraduate academic program in at least three decades. I chaired the committee, which included 30 faculty, 8 students, and 4 recent alumni deployed in four working groups. I also wrote the final report, though its thinking was emphatically a collaborative product—as all good ideas in universities inevitably are. The selection reprinted is a small sample of the Committee's thinking. The full report proposed changes in science, international, and arts education that will significantly strengthen Yale College, as well as long-overdue reforms to undergraduate advising. The full text of the report, which was issued in April 2003, is available online at *www.yale.edu/cyce*.

Introduction

YALE COLLEGE education has changed dramatically throughout its history, and this report seeks to make further changes. Nevertheless, as the context for these innovations, we begin by affirming the philosophy of education that Yale has long embraced. The notion is familiar but is worth a brief review.

Liberal arts education aims to train a broadly based, highly disciplined intelligence without specifying in advance what that intelligence will be used for. In many parts of the world, a student's entry into higher education coincides with the choice of a field or profession, and the function of education is to provide training for this profession. A liberal arts approach differs from that model in at least three ways. First, it regards college as a phase of exploration, a place for the exercise of curiosity and the discovery of new interests and abilities, not the development of interests fully determined in advance. Second, though it permits (even requires) a measure of focus, liberal arts education aims at a significant breadth of preparation, storing the mind with various knowledge and training it in various modes of inquiry rather than building strength in one form alone.

Third and most fundamentally, liberal arts education does not aim to train a student in the particulars of a given career. Instead its goal is to develop deep skills that people can bring to bear in whatever work they eventually choose. These skills include but are not confined to:

> the ability to subject the world to active and continuing curiosity and to ask interesting questions;

> the ability to set a newly noticed fact in a larger field of information, to amass relevant knowledge from a variety of sources and bring it to bear in thoughtful, discerning ways;

> the ability to subject an object of inquiry to sustained and disciplined analysis, and where needed, to more than one mode of analysis;

> the ability to link and integrate frames of reference, creating perceptions that were not available through a single lens;

> the ability to express one's thoughts precisely and persuasively;

> the ability to take the initiative and mobilize one's intelligence without waiting for instructions from others;

> the ability to work with others in such a way as to construct the larger vision no one could produce on his own;

> the sense of oneself as a member of a larger community, local and global, and the sense that one's powers are to be used for the larger good.

Liberal arts education is an old idea and may even seem an old-fashioned one. But a year's reflection has led to the conclusion that this education not only is not passé but may bear even greater value in the future than it has in the past.

We cannot be confident what the coming world will contain, but we can be sure that it will be characterized by increasing complexity, increasing interaction of once-distant cultures and once-distinct forces, increasingly rapid transformations of knowledge, and the continual emergence of new, unforeseen challenges and opportunities. What we must want for our students is that, in the unforeseeable succession of worlds they will live to inhabit, they will be able to summon the powers of mind to understand (and help others understand) this continually emerging reality and to see how to act in it in creative, thoughtful ways. In our judgment, the student best equipped for this future will be a person fitted with multiple skills that can be brought to bear in versatile ways on changing situations: a person who keeps finding new uses for things already learned and keeps gaining new learning from the new facts he or she encounters.

A school of Yale's character is particularly well suited for training of this sort. We note in passing that the formal academic program, the focus of this report, is only one aspect of the schooling Yale provides. Yale College's richly elaborated world of extracurricular activity – in community service and public affairs, in the arts, in sports, journalism, and so on – is another scene of education, an exercise ground where habits of initiative, service, discipline, and working together in groups receive vital elaboration. Beyond that, the very texture of daily life in the undergraduate community is an agent of education. The free-flowing interaction with contemporaries similar to oneself in talent and energy but different in background and outlook has a powerful capacity to open, enliven, and stretch the mind. The spirited, inclusive community grounded in the residential colleges is Yale's great training ground in living and working together in a heterogeneous society, an ethical education grounded in the realities of daily life. Everything Yale does to strengthen this community serves to improve the learning we afford.

Turning back to formal study, a school of Yale's institutional character – a research university where the college is surrounded by a constellation of graduate and professional schools — offers special benefits as a site for liberal arts education. By virtue of its scale, a research university can offer a far larger number of intellectual opportunities than would be available in a liberal arts college. The teachers at a school like Yale are not only active in research but typically preeminent in their fields, and this has further benefits for undergraduates. At such a school, intellectual discovery is not a distant activity or spectator sport. Students study in an environment where knowledge is being not just transmitted but created, and where they can be partners in the unfolding of new understanding.

But along with such benefits, a research university will always have potential downsides as a scene of liberal arts education. In many schools of this character, research agendas can be so compelling as to minimize the attention faculty are willing to pay to undergraduate teaching. The tight specializations fostered by graduate training and research careers can also lead faculty to focus on their parts of the intellectual landscape, with the larger educational whole receiving scant attention. At their best, the research and the liberal arts agendas of a university can be wonderfully complementary, with research creating an excitement that animates the teacher in the classroom, and teaching requiring clarity of communication and a sense of larger bearings with clear benefit to research. But these agendas are not inevitably harmonious, and care is required to make these goals mutually supportive.

Yale has kept undergraduate education much closer to the center of its enterprise than is the case at most comparable universities. This is a place where virtually no faculty member is exempted from the teaching of undergraduates. More positively (and more impressively), it is a place where faculty, including many of the most distinguished scholars, take considerable trouble with the intellectual development of their students. But to say this is not to say that our success is uniform or guaranteed. The competing priorities of the university require constant balancing, and mindfulness of all the ends to be served.

The central recommendation of this report is that Yale

work to maintain and, where needed, to strengthen its commitment to undergraduate education as an inseparable part of its mission as a research university. It would be an impoverishment for undergraduates if Yale were to weaken its commitment to research, the source of so much intellectual vitality and opportunity. It is a value, not a limit, of this school that undergraduates can advance to the frontiers of discovery in virtually every field of study by the end of their undergraduate years. But for the expertise of the faculty to bear its full advantage, the University needs to emphasize that sharing knowledge is a crucial complement to creating and refining it.

To this end, the Committee on Yale College Education reaffirms the central place of teaching in the Faculty of Arts and Sciences. If superiority of scholarly accomplishment is necessary for faculty appointments at Yale, excellence in teaching must also be given substantial weight in all hiring and promotion decisions. The University's high expectations about both teaching and scholarship should be made clear when new members join the faculty. We urge that Yale take as great pains to support the teaching aspirations of its faculty as it does their research activities, and that Yale celebrate outstanding teaching and scholarship in every possible way.

After consulting with faculty, students, administrators, and alumni, we have converged on a list of places where, in our judgment, undergraduate education could be most significantly improved. While maintaining and nourishing existing strengths, we propose that Yale adopt as goals to:

> assure that the educational ambitions of Yale College are clearly articulated, reflected in a curriculum that fully serves these ambitions, and consciously embraced by students as they put their academic programs together;

> sustain and strengthen a culture of close intellectual contact between faculty and students;

> foster the existing disciplines as means to knowledge while supporting forms of inquiry that lie outside or between these disciplines, requiring knowledge to be combined in new ways;

strengthen education in the sciences;

enhance the international dimension of Yale College education;

increase opportunities for the study of the arts including through creative practice;

improve academic advising, especially in the years before the choice of a major.

Our report elaborates on these goals and proposes a variety of means to achieve them.

Distributional Requirements

The Committee did not set out with the principal purpose of reforming Yale College distributional requirements. Nevertheless, our inquiries revealed that current requirements inadvertently contribute to major problems in Yale College education. We therefore think it necessary to make changes – and we believe that if the whole of our recommendation is enacted, undergraduate education will be strikingly improved.

After the elective system was introduced into American colleges and universities, virtually all schools recognized the need to guard against two dangers that it created: education by incoherent, dilettantish smatterings and excessive narrowness of concentration. Early in the 20th century, virtually all colleges wrote two new sets of rules to govern the elective system, one to guarantee depth of education, the other breadth. The first of these, the idea that students should become deeply initiated into the rigors of some intellectual discipline, found expression in the idea of a major concentration; the second led to a mandated distribution of study outside the major area. It is a striking fact that, while the idea of a major has been almost universally adopted and changed little over many decades, breadth requirements have enjoyed no such consensus. Excellent schools have given very different answers to the question how breadth should be assured. Brown has no formal requirements;

Columbia, a required great books core; Harvard, a core that mandates certain kinds of intellectual encounters with a fixed array of classes that fulfill the requirements. Duke has just inaugurated ambitious general studies requirements combining specified areas of knowledge, modes of inquiry, focused inquiries, and competencies.

Through the 1960s, Yale College identified eight areas in which study had to be pursued up to a certain level, which advanced placement work in high school was allowed to satisfy. Yale did away with all breadth requirements in the late 1960s and replaced them with the "Guidelines for the Distribution of Studies" reprinted in the Yale College Programs of Study since that date. In the late 1970s, the faculty adopted the current system of distributional requirements, the demands of which were further fortified in the 1980s. The current requirements are that a student must complete no fewer than 12 courses from outside the distribution group of his or her major; that at least three credits must be earned within each of the four distribution groups; and that for a student whose major lies in Group I (languages and literatures), II (other humanities), or III (social sciences), at least two of the three course credits in group IV must be earned in the natural sciences (not, that is, "in mathematical, applied mathematical, or computational courses"). Students are also required to demonstrate competence in a foreign language at the intermediate level.

The peculiar logic of the Yale distributional requirements is that while they mandate breadth, they allow great freedom as to how this breadth is to be achieved. Unlike core curricula, the Yale system dictates what kind of thing students must study while leaving them free to find the particular course by which to satisfy this obligation. A generation later, the Committee on Yale College Education remains firmly committed to this philosophy. In our view, however desirable it is in theory to say that students should know certain things, whenever something is mandated, there is a cost to the learning obtained. Students end up taking a course in order to meet the requirement rather than from authentic personal interest, with sometimes deadly results for involvement and class atmosphere. We believe that when students have chosen their courses, they are almost inevitably more engaged in them—a first precondition for serious learning. We believe the Yale system gives adequate structure while allowing for the play of exploration and individual curiosity: another prime educational value.

Nevertheless, the Yale distribution system has flaws whose consequences are not trivial. Except for foreign languages, the current system remains almost spectacularly vague about the skills it expects students to build strength in, freeing them to avoid their weaknesses in ways that can prove seriously self-impoverishing. The failure to be specific about skills as distinct from subject fields also means that the requirements can be fulfilled in ways that make little sense: a student can currently fulfill the Group I requirement by taking two terms of introductory language classes and one term of first-level expository writing, but that hardly seems the exposure to the Humanities the requirement intended. (The odd wrinkle about computational courses suggests another unarticulated distinction between skills and substantive fields.) Further, in the most blatant failure of the current system, whether a course counts for satisfying a distributional requirement is now a function of the instructor's departmental appointment, not its particular intellectual content. When this is coupled with the relative scarcity of science classes available to nonscientists and the competition nonscientists fear from students who might have a leg up on them, it creates a perverse incentive to satisfy the science requirement by seeking the courses designated Group IV with the least scientific content. The problem of Yale science education cannot be solved while the rule remains in effect.

The Committee weighed many alternatives in approaching these problems. We noted with interest the effort of other schools to frame requirements that articulate all the things they want students to learn: research skills, ethical reasoning, cross-cultural inquiry, and many more. We chose against such a course, not because we think these goals are unimportant (far from it), but because we are not persuaded that the multiplication of mandated categories is the way to produce a deeply engaged, broadly informed mind. Education is not like a recipe, where the desired outcome is produced by adding fixed quantities of discrete ingredients to the mix; nor do students make the most interesting use of educational opportunities when they are preoccupied with checking off the boxes.

Balancing our desire to promote exploration and intellectual engagement with the need for trained competence and broad exposure, we propose the following revisions:

> In place of the current requirements, students will be required to take no fewer than two courses in the Humanities and Arts, two courses in the Social Sciences, and two courses in the Natural Sciences. In addition, they will also be required to take two courses in any field that give attention to the development of writing skills; two courses in any field that strengthen skills in quantitative reasoning and analysis; and such work as will allow them to attain competence in a foreign language at the intermediate level, or, if they have already reached it, to build their skills further. In doubtful cases, courses will be designated as meeting these requirements by the relevant curricular review bodies based on their content and educational ambitions, not the affiliation of the instructor.

We hasten to add several comments.

First and most obviously, the proposed requirements constitute our idea of a minimal education, not an adequate one. They are a rough, schematic representation of the least that an educated person should seek to know. They are to be embraced as starting points, not goals.

Second, though we do not view education as the acquisition of some finite set of competences, we regard certain skills as sufficiently foundational that Yale should single them out for conscious attention. These powers hold the key to many things students will want to be able to know and do in later study and later life. People who fail to develop them at an early stage are limiting their futures without knowing what opportunities they are shutting down. As a result, we believe that students should not only develop these powers but should make this development an intentional goal of their college education. This is the aim of the requirements.

We also think it important that undergraduates travel some further distance in these skills however accomplished they may have become in high school. These competences mature and deepen: the best high school writer still has a way to go to become the writer he or she could be. Further, when the development of these powers stops with high school, the result can be a going backward, not a standing still. Students who do not use their math or foreign language skills in college commonly lose abilities they once had and can graduate knowing less than when they arrived.

We would require further work, then, both of those who obviously need it and those who seemingly don't. But we want to be clear about the form of work we have in mind. It is emphatically not our wish to require students to take any particular course as the way to satisfy these requirements. We believe that this sort of instruction should be widely disseminated throughout the Yale College curriculum, such that a student could choose a course in any number of subjects for its independent interest, and still receive training in the skill in question. Though we applaud the English Department for teaching expository writing, it is not our intent to require each Yale College student to take a course in expository writing. Rather than isolating this study from the rest of education, we envision serious writing training as being available in scores of courses in many disciplines, in the Humanities, in the Social Sciences, and ideally in the Sciences as well, such that it could be integral to and receive reinforcement from a student's whole program of study.

The quantitative reasoning requirement aims to increase student appreciation and command of numerical representation and its cognates. The mental rigor that results from this study has been celebrated for as long as formal education has existed. In addition, in modern times, applications of quantitative methods have proved critical to an astonishingly wide range of disciplines. Here again, however, it is not our idea to require any particular class in any particular department. The Math, Statistics, and Computer Science Departments would make obvious contributions to such teaching, but students would also be able to fulfill this goal in appropriate courses in Physics, Chemistry, Geology, Astronomy, and the various Biology and Engineering departments, and in Psychology, Economics, Political Science, and Sociology as well.

Further, to satisfy the aims we have in mind, these changes in the distributional requirements have to be made in tandem with other changes. Satisfying a set of requirements never produced a good education, however enlightened the requirements. An academic obligation is only as good the intellectual opportunities available for fulfilling it; and even then, its value will depend on whether a student is meeting the spirit or the letter of the law. For the new requirements to work, Yale must consciously strengthen the instruction it gives in the skills in question across wide areas of the curriculum. Quite as important, for these requirements to be successful, they must be implemented together with advising that can make these competences into actively pursued educational goals.

In thinking about this matter, the Committee was struck by something recently built in our midst. Some years ago, Yale College addressed the question of how to strengthen foreign language instruction. Yale had traditionally left such programs to the many separate departments of language and literature. But this arrangement left language instructors in different programs severely isolated from one another, and it left program quality at the mercy of each department's degree of interest in language pedagogy. Taking elementary language instruction out of the departments and locating it in its own administrative center, as some universities have done, held out the possibility of helping with these problems but created problems of its own: in particular, it broke the vital link between introductory teaching and higher-level language uses.

With help from the Mellon Foundation, Yale pioneered a different model. We kept these programs as integral components of their departments but gave them supplementary support through a newly created Center for Language Study. In complement to the departments, this Center has created a community among language teachers; supplied a place where shared issues of language pedagogy can be addressed; offered incentives for curricular experiment and support (including technological support) for new teaching practices; and provided a way to keep in touch with enlightened developments outside of Yale.

We urge that similar centers be created in support of the other areas highlighted in the new requirements. It is essential that that they be equipped with adequate resources to fulfill these teaching missions. To be more particular:

The Committee recommends the establishment of an expanded version of the current Bass Writing Program to support writing instruction across the curriculum. We recommend that this program be strengthened along the lines proposed in the Report of the Committee on Writing Instruction, which was warmly received by the Yale College faculty in November 2002. The Center would help faculty rethink the writing components of their courses whatever the discipline, supporting this task through workshops, grants, and consulting services. The Center would also administer an amplified version of the current writing tutor program tailored to student needs and to needs in specific courses or clusters of courses. The Committee is eager for undergraduates to improve their abilities in speaking as well as writing. This Center would be the base from which to strengthen skills in oral communication as well.

We also call for the creation of a center to support the teaching of quantitative reasoning. Like the Center for Foreign Language Study and the Bass Writing Program, the QR Center would not supplant the role of departments but would supply what no department can realistically manage on its own. Many existing courses would already meet the new Q requirement, and many more could meet it if they made this aspect of instruction a more conscious goal. At present, however, there is no way to highlight this goal or to give teachers support in meeting it. In addition, beyond already adequate courses and revisions of existing courses, we will almost certainly need further curricular developments if we are to boost the quantitative skills of all undergraduates. But as of now, there is no place for seeing this area of instruction whole and spotting what further might be needed.

Supported by a faculty council and staffed with appropriate pedagogical and technological expertise, the QR Center would draw faculty from disparate disciplines together around shared pedagogical concerns, providing a place for the exchange of good ideas, offering incentives for curricular innovation, and supporting course improvement and new course creation with appropriate dedicated resources. Given its perspective on larger instructional needs, the Center would also be in a position to second departmental requests for incremental faculty resources to meet this educational aim. The Center would also administer an extensive tutoring program to help students of all abilities meet the challenges of this form of learning and would advocate for classroom needs in quantitative areas. The outfitting of classrooms with appropriate computer support and projection equipment will be an important part of this initiative. The Center would work in close alliance with other forces promoting the teaching of quantitative reasoning: the faculty cooperating on unified Statistics training for social and natural science majors, the staff of the Statistics Lab, the Director of Math Instruction in the Math Department, and so on.

We regard such teaching support to be integral to the success of the new distributional system. It is not our thought to send students to meet new requirements solely from existing courses: this Committee has the profound conviction that academic requirements only work when they are accompanied by an ample array of well-conceived, compellingly taught courses in which to satisfy these goals. The new requirements and the means to meet the requirements must come into existence at the same time. As soon as the faculty endorses the new system, appropriate committees should be convened to designate courses for the new distributional requirements and to advise on areas of needed development. Once the new requirements are passed and courses begin to be designated in the needed ways, students should be permitted to meet either the requirements they entered with or the new requirements if they so choose. We urge that the new requirements be made mandatory by the time the Class of 2009 enters in the fall of 2005. This will give the faculty two years to take the necessary curricular steps.

Finally, some further remarks on the foreign language requirement. The study of languages has long been understood to be one of the rudiments of a liberal arts education. The benefits of language study include (but are not limited to) increased understanding of how languages work, often resulting in heightened sophistication in the use of one's own language; unmediated access to texts otherwise available only in translation, or not at all; and the ability to cross cultural barriers by being able to communicate across linguistic bounds. In the internationalized world of the 21st century, this form of education will become yet more important. To participate fully in a global society, students will need to be able to enter into profoundly different cultural settings and communicate across cultural lines.

With these thoughts in mind, the Committee reaffirms the centrality of foreign language study to undergraduate education but proposes certain modifications to the requirement. We continue to believe that serious command of a foreign language takes more than a single year of study. At present, a student is able to satisfy the foreign language requirement by achieving an appropriate advanced placement score, or by passing an examination at Yale, or by passing intermediate-level courses in a foreign language at Yale. In order to promote firsthand experience in foreign cultures and the learning of language in real-world settings, the Committee recommends that students be allowed to satisfy the foreign language requirement by completing the introductory level of language instruction in the classroom and then completing an approved summer study or internship in a foreign language–speaking setting abroad.

For this recommendation to work, the University must significantly expand its ability to help undergraduates locate suitable international opportunities. More detailed remarks on this issue follow later in the report. As we promote international experience as a way to fulfill the language requirement, it will also be important that students plan these parts of their program in a thoughtful, foresightful way. In our ideal scenario, students electing a foreign language class in the freshman year would already be thinking how they might follow it up with an experience abroad the following summer, and how they could build on that learning in later coursework.

Finally, we have noted our belief that, whatever their attainments before coming here, students should travel some further distance in developing foundational skills in the course of their college years. We believe that it makes better educational sense to set Yale's language requirement in these terms than in terms of a fixed point to be reached. For students who arrive at Yale without demonstrable language skills, the Committee recommends that three terms of foreign language (rather than the current four) suffice to meet the foreign language requirement, or two terms followed by a suitable experience abroad. This will require a considerable "distance traveled" for them while also recognizing the value of other educational opportunities and priorities: when students require four terms of coursework to meet the requirement, they must spend one-sixth of the credits required for graduation in introductory or intermediate foreign language instruction. For students who arrive at Yale with the equivalent of one, two, or three terms of language competence, the current requirements will continue to apply, with the new international option added.

Many students have enough previous study to pass the current language requirement upon arrival, and some students with a native language other than English pass the requirement by that means. Because of the complex and continuing benefits of language study, however, we recommend that all students be required to engage in some form of postsecondary language study regardless of the level achieved at the time of matriculation. Students who can show intermediate-level competence in a foreign language upon arrival would have several options by which to meet this requirement. They could enroll in a one-semester course that further advances their linguistic training in the same language, for instance a course in literature or culture. (This may require innovative course development at the appropriate levels.) Or, by special arrangement with the instructor and the DUS of the relevant foreign language program, they could extend their competence by completing a significant portion of the work of a regular Yale course using their foreign language in place of English. Or they could undertake an approved experience abroad in a country where their language is spoken. Alternatively, they might begin the study of another language. All that would not be permitted would be to make no further use of language acquisitions during the college years. A student for whom English is a second language could demonstrate the "distance traveled" by doing further work in English or studying another foreign language.

FORMS OF FAREWELL

BACCALAUREATE READINGS

In Yale College, Commencement begins with a baccalaureate service held in Woolsey Hall, which also supplied the scene for the graduates' Freshman Assembly. On this occasion, as Dean I read a few short passages, varied year by year, with some attendant commentary. This is a representative selection, from May 2002.

FOUR YEARS AGO, when this place was in no sense yet your home, we gathered in this room to welcome you to your new home. Four years later, when this school truly has become your home, we regather to prepare to evict you. For your graduation present, the English teacher in me revives to offer four short passages of verse, lines that I hope might capture some of the moods of this occasion.

First I wanted to capture the way your life here could have been so intensely real and yet so transient, as it prepares to vanish behind you. For this I have reached into the work of one of my favorite living poets, Marie Borroff, the first woman to earn tenure at Yale. This poem takes off from an experience easy to replicate in New Haven: walking downhill on Prospect Street as undergraduates trudge up that street to classes on Science Hill, and, while seeing them, hearing the bells from St. Mary's Church on Hillhouse Avenue as they chime the hour. In the poem, such simultaneous hearing makes the experience of seeing be a seeing in the prospect of time: a seeing of everything both in its presence and in the prospect of its evanescence. The poem is called "In Range of Bells."

I walk in range of bells,
  where silence (one by one)
    marks off each stroke that tells
      time ended, time begun.

Daily down Prospect Hill
  the tally keeps (nine, ten)
    telling with what a constant will
      time brings me round and round again,

and brings me schoolward here
  to breast the advancing line:
    eyes, faces year by year
      young, and more young than mine,

while bell on bell, borne past
  as leaves blow from a tree,
    tell how time's branches hold us fast
      only to cast us free.

Next I wanted to capture the sense that the regret and loss produced by departure could be joined with a shadow of possible gain, an apprehension of what might lie ahead — and of the interest of what might lie ahead — in a still-obscure future. Here I read from the first recorded experience of departure, that of your famous ancestors Adam and Eve, who, like you, went to a great place but eventually had to leave it, although, unlike you, they failed to graduate. I read from Milton's *Paradise Lost*:

Some natural tears they dropp'd, but wip'd them soon;
The World was all before them, where to choose
Thir place of rest, and Providence their guide;
They hand in hand with wand'ring steps and slow,
Through Eden took thir solitary way.

Now as you leave, you will have (or will feel you should have) goals, life-destinations you feel you should aim for. So someone should tell you that the point of life-goals is not altogether to reach them, but partly to open up a space for effort and exploration, an interesting experience along the way. Here I read from a poem (somewhat shortened for the occasion) by the Greek poet C. P. Cavafy, with its suggestion that the real point of Odysseus's journey was not to get home: instead, having the goal of getting home created the possibility of the journey. This is from Cavafy's "Ithaka."

> As you set out for Ithaka
> hope the voyage is a long one,
> full of adventure, full of discovery.
> Laistrygonians and Cyclops,
> angry Poseidon – don't be afraid of them:
> you'll never find things like that on your way
> as long as you keep your thoughts raised high,
> as long as a rare excitement
> stirs your spirit and your body.
>
> Hope the voyage is a long one,
> May there be many a summer morning when,
> with what pleasure, what joy,
> you come into harbors seen for the first time;
> may you stop at Phoenician trading stations
> to buy fine things,
> and may you visit many Egyptian cities
> to gather stores of knowledge from their scholars.
>
> Keep Ithaka always in your mind.
> Arriving there is what you are destined for.
> But do not hurry the journey at all.
> Better if it lasts for years,
> so you are old by the time you reach the island,
> wealthy with all you have gained on the way,
> not expecting Ithaka to make you rich.
>
> Ithaka gave you the marvelous journey,
> Without her you would not have set out.
> She has nothing left to give you now.

And if you find her poor, Ithaka won't have fooled you.
Wise as you will have become, so full of experience,
you will have understood by then what these Ithakas mean.

Last, though your graduation marks the end point of your college life, your goal here was not to graduate. Your goal was to get the good of this place: to make something more of yourself, in preparation to make yet more of yourself — then yet more, then yet more — in the course of your later life. In this sense, your college years aren't a home you are losing but more like a draft, a draft being, you will remember, not something intended to be perfect, but work done to enable the development of something more perfect later on. This put me in mind of these words from Melville's *Moby-Dick*, which I offer as my last gift:

> God keep me from ever completing anything. This whole book is but a draught — nay, but a draught of a draught. Oh, Time, Strength, Cash, and Patience!

Let's review. This college may have had a hold on you, but its aim was not to hold you. Its aim was to hold you for a while, then to cast you free — as we do now. When this chapter of life closes behind you, at that moment, the world will be all before you. I wish you good goals, goals that will yield a full and productive life on the way to them, whether reached or not. And I wish you time, strength, cash, and patience as you advance toward them. Providence be your guide.

SINGING IN THE
PROSPECT OF TIME

For the Yale tercentennial, my classmate Richard Nash Gould, now
an architect but long a noted singer, prepared a visual history of Yale in
the 20th century focused around Yale's most famous *a cappella* group,
the Whiffenpoofs. He asked me to contribute a short preface. This
was an occasion to reflect not just on the role of music in college but
on the meaning of extracurricular activity in general, and on a yet
deeper feature of college life: its logic of evanescence. From *Yale College,
The Twentieth Century: A History in Present Time* (forthcoming).

OUR MEMORIES are what they are. Each of us has the memories we have, and not others. Through the chances of biography, my first Whiffenpoof memory comes from September or
October 1964, the fall of my freshman year, when one of my
roommates, Eugene Lyman, brought a recent Whiffenpoofs
record back to our Wright Hall suite. He had bought it, I suppose, in a burst of school spirit, or possibly in the thought that it
would help us acculturate ourselves to the Yale milieu. But in a
room more attuned to the early Beatles and early Dylan, the
Whiffenpoofs' harmonies sounded at first a little quaint, and
the notion that people might have an authentic preference for
such music seemed far-fetched, to say the least.

In days when the young did not own a million recordings,
however, this album was played and replayed, and before long I
found myself not just knowing the songs but even, somewhat
against my better judgment, liking them, and unconsciously
incorporating them into my mental world. It's for this reason
that I could to this day, if pressed, sing the entirety of this long-

lost LP, which introduced me to songs and kinds of songs I had not previously known. This album taught me a song whose words seemed only slightly less retro in 1964 than they do today but whose upbeat mood and absurdly insistent rhyme scheme made it oddly delightful:

> My cutie's due
> On the two two two
> She's coming in
> On the old choo choo . . .

In another vein, there was melancholy so melodious as to make misery itself seem like an object of desire:

> When Sunny gets blue,
> Her eyes get gray and cloudy,
> Then the rain begins to fall . . .

Or, in a song long vanished from the repertoire (one understands why), there was the note of cocky swagger, derived, one imagined, from the gentlemen songsters' sprees:

> If I could do inspirationally
> What I mostly do mechanically,
> All the girls would do spontaneously
> What they always do eventually.

I recite fragments of this memory not because I believe my own Whiffenpoofian primal scene to be so significant but because all Yalies will have their own versions of such a memory. If it is correct to say that the Whiffenpoofs are a Yale institution, what this means is that their music has entered into the life of this place. One can like that sort of thing or not, care about it a lot or a little, but the singing the Whiffs epitomize is a more or less inescapable part of the Yale environment. This is one of the experiences Yale alumni hold in common. To have gone to Yale is to have had such music in one's ears.

But what does it mean that the Whiffenpoofs should be

one of the most persistent expressions of Yale College culture? To the eyes of the Dean, part of the answer lies in the group's paradigmatic quality, its representativeness not just of the larger *a cappella* scene but of the whole manic world of organized activity that is such a distinctive Yale College feature. Tocqueville thought that the love of voluntary associations was one of the most striking characteristics of American life, and if he could have visited modern Yale he would have found the epicenter of this phenomenon. From its endless dramatic and instrumental groups to its wildly proliferating student newspapers, magazines, and journals to its nearly uncountable community service organizations, environmental action groups, political debating societies, and varsity, club, and intramural sports teams, Yale is the natural home of group activity, with the Whiffenpoofs, in every way except their lack of women, a kind of the emblem of the whole.

In this group as in others, students with demanding academic programs use their free time to impose extensive further demands upon themselves. (As with many extracurricular activities, the Dean does not want to know how many hours a week it takes to be a Whiffenpoof.) Not just do they engage in a time-consuming activity. In doing so students push themselves toward new levels of excellence, embracing the discipline needed to turn a knack into a high-level skill. But if they have elements of work and striving, groups like the Whiffenpoofs are also scenes of heightened pleasure, places where students experience the joy of using their talents, the joy of offering the spectacle of their talents to others, and the joy of accomplishing together what no one of them could achieve alone.

We speak of such activities as extracurricular, but if singing groups and their cognates have a central place at Yale it is because they further the education we have in mind to offer. As much as anything in the formal academic curriculum, they put central Yale values into practice: values like the belief that to have a gift is to have an obligation to use it well, for instance, or belief in the importance of living in and working for the benefit of a community.

If the Whiffs have special standing among extracurricular groups, it's partly because they exemplify these values so clearly. A Whiffenpoofs performance is invariably a display of highly developed individual talent, but also, beyond that, of the greater wholes individuals can make when they act in concert. But if it is representative in some sense, the Whiffs, like every undergraduate organization, have a distinctive character, which in this case is not hard to name.

The special quality this group cultivates is a suave traditionalism. In the down-market world of modern student fashion, the Whiffs dress like gentlemen of the old school in their signature white tie and tails. Their style of harmony is similarly noncontemporary, as is their repertoire itself. "My Cutie's Due" and "When Sunny Gets Blue" were songs of an older day when they were sung as Whiffenpoof staples in the 1960s. Beloved popular songs of my youth, "On Broadway" and "Midnight Train to Georgia," entered the Whiff repertoire and became staples in turn, but not until they had taken on a patina of age. The ravishingly beautiful "Time After Time," by my classmate Bob Birge, was a new tune of the late '60s, but it did not sound like one. It is now sung by undergraduates for whom its origins are lost in the mists of time.

To the uninitiated, the Whiffenpoof style runs the risk of seeming snobbish and anachronistic. But to "get" the Whiffenpoofs is to understand that they are not reactionary in any simple or familiar sense. The members are always spirited young men fully at home in contemporary culture, which means that their style is not the expression of their inward natures but a performance, a way of acting they have chosen to put on. And they clearly give the sense that they have embraced this style not as a tribute to some idealized, piously embraced old order, still less for the campy fun of parodying vanished gentility, but because an unusual coolness and beauty can still be produced through these forms: the fact each performance aims to prove anew.

It remains true, however, that their manner is heavily evocative of the past, and this has an important further effect. When the Whiffenpoofs assemble, they perform a sense of history through the action of their song.

Music is always a game played with time, in which time's shapeless successions are re-fashioned into something measured and composed. But if music defeats time by inscribing it in a human order, it is still a thing of time, filling the moment with its beauty without escaping the law of evanescence.

When music insists on its historical origins, its sense of temporality grows deeper and more complex. The chief fact about the Whiffenpoofs is that the members of any moment are always this year's Whiffenpoofs. When they perform, they present themselves as this year's avatars of a long tradition, dressed this year as their predecessors dressed in past years, singing this year the songs others sang before. The effect is to emphasize not mere repetition but rather the cooperation of generations across time. In its emphatic traditionalism, this music reminds its listeners that others, not the current singers, originated these songs, and that other others have sung them along the way. This is a gesture of recognition toward the past, but it also conveys the message that the days of those others are indeed past: they sang these songs in their time, but they are not around to sing them now. On the other hand, through this singing, something in one sense over and done with manages to live on, by recruiting fresh hands to the game. Received across time, the sounds past groups made give each present cohort the means for their expression. And as the past enables the present, the present revivifies the past. That older singing seems over and gone, until fresh voices sing it back to splendid life.

But this is not the whole of what the singing says. For the temporal perspective this music opens out carries the further message that the singers before our eyes, so very present to us and so full of life, will prove no less transient than their predecessors. In case we missed the point, their theme song proclaims it:

We will serenade our Louis
While voice and life shall last,
Then we'll pass and be forgotten with the rest.

I have tried to suggest how the Whiffenpoofs are like other campus groups, and in a sense they are. But in the intensity with which they give off this message the Whiffs are like no other group at all. If there is something centrally "Yale" about them, it is because the sense of time they express resonates with the deepest fact of college life, indeed of life itself. Every student who has passed through this school has had the same sensation for most of their Yale careers: So what if other people went here? This is our place, the scene of our vitality! But toward the end the truth comes clear. We are to be here for a time only, and the same current that brought us to our college years will now lead us beyond them — to be replaced, in new times, by new young folk, whose energy, talent, and friendship will give new life to our past enterprise, then make way for others in their turn.

Yale College, the Twentieth Century, to my mind the most remarkable of many that have marked the Yale tercentennial, is a powerful reflection on this fact. Only minimally a history of the Whiffenpoofs, in reality it is a history of Yale College in the 20th century. But it is not a work of generalized narrative history. Rather, it is a book of Yale life, registering, year by year, the things that happened when that time was present time, with the look and feel of life itself. Thanks to the compiler's endless care, unmatched archival labors, and extraordinary visual sense, each page of this volume retrieves the forgotten life of past moments, in pictures that read less like records of events than bursts of recovered vitality. But each page, however absorbing, is also only a page, succeeded by another, then another — so the book itself teaches a lesson in time's ways.

Like the singing it celebrates, this book captures the way humans fill the fleeting present with their energies, the way life slips from life into the past, and the way it can be revived and extended in the new life of others — year after year, time after time, as in a school, as in the world. For teaching this lesson in so rich a form, we owe an immense debt to Richard Nash Gould.

REMARKS ON ACCEPTING
THE PRESIDENCY
OF DUKE UNIVERSITY

Delivered at the Perkins Library, Duke University, December 12, 2003

I THANK YOU all for this exceptionally warm welcome. When you know me you won't often find me at a loss for words, but you'll pardon me if I'm a little overwhelmed. This is one of the great moments of my life.

Let me tell you a true story. I had been brought down to Durham, in thick disguise, for a final stealth interview last Friday, and since there was a blizzard going on where I come from, my trip home was complex. I could only fly as far as Washington, and in my circuitous journey from that point forward, I had a long cab ride. The cabbie—an Afghan immigrant—was very affable and interesting and we fell to talking. After a while, he said, "If you don't mind my asking, what do you do?" "I'm a college professor," I told him, in my usual discreet and unrevealing way. Without losing a beat he replied, "Oh! It's the dream of my life that my daughters will go to Duke."

Hearing this was like getting an electric shock. This man, a total stranger and random specimen of humanity, could have had no idea where I was coming from or what I had on my mind. But Duke was in *his* mind, though he had absolutely no connection to it, and on his mind as what? A name for something excellent; a name for something to aspire to; a name for a place that would open the door to knowledge and all the life opportunities that education can provide. I hope that man's

217

daughters do come here. But you know what? By the time I was in that cab, it had also become my dream to attach myself to this university and all its meanings and promise. Lucky me! It came to pass. I've been admitted to Duke, and I'm coming.

This has been a big decision for me, as big as any in my life. Let me say a word about how I came to it. I was not restless. I was not looking for a job. I've had a wonderful life at a great institution. I may be America's least disaffected employee. Yale has been a great place to teach, my first and most abiding passion; also a great place to do my scholarly work and pursue my intellectual life; and my current job has given me a thousand challenges and opportunities for what I care for most: strengthening the work of education. When I was first contacted by your committee, however, my curiosity was piqued. Duke is one of the handful of top universities in the world, after all, and if I went anywhere, it would only be to somewhere like that. So I entered into discussions, and under your committee's skillful tutelage, I came to have a clearer and clearer sense of this place. You already know it, but let me try to tell you what this stranger and outsider saw.

First, Duke is a university with the feel and human scale of a small school but the intellectual resources of a big school, with a college anchoring a full array of outstanding professional schools. Second, and this is rarer than you may recognize, Duke is a university whose different schools and centers and departments not only coexist but actually interact, and even like to interact. I've been to a lot of universities in my day, but I've never been to one where there was such a powerful sense of interschool and interdisciplinary collaboration, and of the special dynamism such interactions can breed.

Third, and I felt this very powerfully, Duke is a young school that has managed to raise itself into the top ranks in fairly short time but that manifestly continues to rise and to want to rise. When I took my stealth tour, I loved your campus, which is so beautiful in a traditional way, but what I really loved was the coexistence of tradition and heady forward progress: all those cranes towering over the Gothic buildings, saying that the building phase at Duke is something of the present and future, not just the past. I was particularly floored by those great modern research facilities hidden just behind the west campus quad. They show that this is a school capable of having major aspirations and seeing them through – plus at Duke, all that scientific and medical research activity is right next door, where undergraduates can feel its energy and get in on its excitement, not miles away in a separate kingdom.

In the same vein, I found Duke a school with a strong sense of priorities for the future improvement, priorities to my mind quite brilliantly articulated that are proof of your faculty and administration's ability to think and work together on important challenges. I've also felt no defensiveness here about improvement, no desire to treat the status quo as the pinnacle of progress. So it's a school that has come a long way, wants to go farther, and is unusually well positioned to succeed in doing so.

But then, over against all this dynamism and drive, or accompanying it with no sense of contradiction, I also learned that Duke is just an overwhelmingly friendly place, a place full of people who are both very smart and very nice, a place where people appreciate each other, are relaxed around each other, care about and enjoy each other, and have a healthy sense of the good things of life. In addition to the sense of community on campus, it's also a place that takes seriously its role in the community – the community of Durham, the Research Triangle, and North Carolina more generally. If it's true that we live in a knowledge economy, then universities have special things to contribute to the surrounding world, and a special obligation to make those contributions. In Duke I saw a school that wants to be a good citizen in the strong sense of that word, and I believe in that.

Put it all together – what you are and what you want to be – and I must say, it made an impression. A growing impression: I moved, over the course of the last weeks, from being intrigued to deeply interested to quite excited by what I saw here, and I had a stronger and stronger sense of the work to be done here and the fun there might be in doing it. And then came the day when, as Huck Finn said, I had to choose, forever, betwixt two things, and I knowed it: my wonderful life in a known world or the adventure of Duke. Well, you know my choice. I'm a person of strong attachments and powerful devotions who has a lot of energy and wants nothing more than to use that energy on behalf of the deep goals of universities: education, the creation and transmission of knowledge, and the training of the young for constructive lives in the world. It has been my pride to do that work at Yale. Today I transfer my loyalty to this place: from here forward, it will be my honor to do it at Duke. The switch should not be hard. Everything I own is blue, and I am used to four-letter names.

Let me say a few words of thanks. The first is to the search committee and its extraordinary chair, Bob Steel. During the time when I scarcely knew Duke, these folks embodied Duke for me, and they could not have shown it in a more appealing light. They were by turns smart, serious, committed, and fun. What struck me the most was how much they loved Duke and appreciated and admired each other. I could like a place like that, I thought—and here I am. Second, in addition to being wonderfully helpful to me as I tried to get a sense of Duke, Nan Keohane has been a most remarkable President. This is bad for me in one way but good in another. On the one hand, she sets terrible standards for her successor, and I'm sure I will live to regret the many days when people say "When Nan was here" or "If only Nan were here." Thanks, Nan. But far more than that, Nan has helped shape a university where the faculty trusts the administration (and even likes the president) and feels that we are all working toward common goals. I am lucky to inherit that achievement. This time I mean it: thanks, Nan. Third, and here I will not say by any means all that's in my heart, I thank my family—my mother and father, who nourished my education in every way, and my wife and son, who give me strength and joy every step of the way. I'm a person who has had many blessings. My new life at Duke is among the chief of them. But my family is at the heart of them.

Last, to every member of the Duke community, let me say thank you in advance for the work we will do together. People speak of educational leaders, but the main truth about universities is that absolutely nothing happens in them through the strength of one. I bring high hopes to this job, but whatever I accomplish will be accomplished through our common labor and with your constant help. Together, you have made this a great school. Together, let's keep it great and make it better yet. I pledge you my full commitment to Duke and to what we will make Duke through our work together.

The benefit overran the merit the first day,
and has overrun the merit ever since. The merit
itself, so-called, I reckon part of the receiving.
Emerson, "Experience"

A Note on the Type

This is the first book set entirely in Yale,
a typeface commissioned by the Office of
the University Printer and designed
by Matthew Carter of the School of Art.